LET'S LEARN ABOUT...
THE LAND

Teacher's Guide

STEAM

K2

Pearson Education Limited
KAO Two, KAO Park, Harlow, Essex, CM17 9NA, England
and Associated Companies around the world.

© Pearson Education Limited 2020

The right of Luciana Pinheiro and Simara H. Dal'Alba, to be identified as author of this Work has been asserted by them in accordance with the Copyright, Designs and Patents Act 1988.
All rights reserved; no part of this publication may be reproduced, stored in a retrieval system, or transmitted in any form or by any means, electronic, mechanical, photocopying, recording, or otherwise without the prior written permission of the Publishers.

First published 2020

ISBN: 978-1-292-33447-9

Set in Mundo Sans
Printed in China (SWTC/01)

Acknowledgements
The publishers and author(s) would like to thank the following people and institutions for their feedback and comments during the development of the material: Marcos Mendonça, Leandra Dias, Viviane Kirmeliene, Rhiannon Ball, Gisele Aga, Mônica Bicalho and GB Editorial. The publishers would also like to thank all the teachers who contributed to the development of Let's learn about...: Adriano de Paula Souza, Aline Ramos Teixeira Santo, Aline Vitor Rodrigues Pina Pereira, Ana Paula Gomez Montero, Anna Flávia Feitosa Passos Camila Jarola, Celiane Junker Silva, Edegar França Junior, Fabiana Reis Yoshio, Fernanda de Souza Thomaz, Luana da Silva, Michael Iacovino Luidvinavicius, Munique Dias de Melo, Priscila Rossatti Duval Ferreira Neves, Sandra Ferito, and schools that took part in Construindo Juntos.

Author Acknowledgements
Luciana Pinheiro and Simara H. Dal'Alba

Image Credit(s):
Pearson Education Ltd: 7, 8, 10, 14, 16, 16, 20, 20, 22, 24, 26, 28, 40, 45, 52, 56, 60, 62, 66, 70, MRS Editorial 44, 44, 44, 44, Sheila Cabeza de Vaca 65
Shutterstock.com: Akhmad Dody Firmansyah 18, Anatolii Riepin 54, Ann679 38, Art Alex 7, 34, AtlasStudio 18, BaLL LunLa 18, Fetullah Mercan 30, Fotinia 36, Gts 54, Julien Tromeur 42, Karpov Ilia 58, Kyselova Inna 54, Lauritta 42, Mama Belle and the kids 18, MyImages - Micha 18, Mything 42, Nelea33 54, New Africa 54, Sabelskaya 46, Sunnydream 58, Vietnam Stock Images 18, Yevgen Kravchenko 46

Illustration Acknowledgements
Illustrated by Filipe Laurentino and MRS Editorial

Cover illustration © Filipe Laurentino

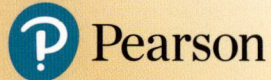

Contents

	Table of contents	4
	Presentation	6
U1	What do you like about yourself?	8
U2	Why do we go to school?	16
U3	How can you help your family at home?	24
U4	Why do we feel hot or cold?	32
U5	What other living things are around us?	40
U6	Why is food important?	48
U7	How can farm animals help us?	56
U8	Who lives and works in my town?	64

Table of contents - STEAM

UNIT	LESSON 1	LESSON 2	LESSON 3	LESSON 4
Unit 1 What do you like about yourself? page 8	• Talk about what germs are and how to avoid spreading them • Follow a sequence in a story • Group items by shape and size • Use soap to make drawings on black paper	• Talk about personal hygiene and their face • Make a "cough not/sneeze not" model of themselves • Think of a solution to reach a high sink	• Talk about hypotheses and hypothetical situations • Understand that *What if* questions are about possibilities, imagination, and creativity • Solve problems in a creative and critical way	• Talk about their body functions • Identify the algorithm of a mindfulness exercise • Learn how to categorize items
Unit 2 Why do we go to school? page 16	• Develop balance, body control, concentration, and posture through dancing • Categorize garbage cans by color and waste as compost or recyclable • Make handmade recycled paper	• Understand why recycling is important • Design recycled toys • Make color patterns out of recyclable paper	• Learn about sounds, music, and rhythm • Measure different amounts of water • Think of ways to make a musical instrument collage using shapes	• Talk about school routines • Spot and debug a problem in a program • Identify the sequence in their school routine • Make a school routine poster and put it in the classroom
Unit 3 How can you help your family at home? page 24	• Talk about movies and how they are made • Understand the logical order in a story through pictures • Learn that old movies were silent • Make a stop motion animation	• Be introduced to the idea that a sharp turn to the right makes our body fall to the left • Follow the steps of an engineering design process: ask, imagine, create, improve, reflect • Fix things to reuse them • Match figures of people doing chores with their outlines	• Learn about ducks' habitat • Count backwards from five to one • Plan, design, and make binoculars • Develop problem-solving skills and introduce computational thinking • Reenact a duck family rhyme	• Encode letters into a binary code • Make a binary bracelet • Order people in a family from the shortest to the tallest • Learn that binary codes are made from ones and zeros and write a letter using binary code • Relate binary code to computer language
Unit 4 Why do we feel hot or cold? page 32	• Improve concentration and the ability to find similarities in colors through a memory game • Understand the concept of light reflection through an experiment • Identify two of the main elements of art: color and texture • Use a technological device to record the results of an experiment (if available)	• Identify different types of weather • Identify different thermometers • Make a thermometer for their classroom • Measure the temperature	• Do an experiment and see how white clothes protect them from heat • Make hypotheses before checking results	• Talk about the colors of leaves • Investigate why leaves change color • Make an artwork by rubbing a crayon on a leaf • Group items by color

UNIT	LESSON 1	LESSON 2	LESSON 3	LESSON 4
Unit 5 What other living things are around us? page 40	• Talk about pollination and make an experiment to see how it works • Work on a sequence to help a bee pollinate flowers • Understand that when the process is not correctly ordered, it might affect the result	• Learn about bees and make a craft bee • Learn that honeycombs are made of hexagon shapes • Count the hexagons in a honeycomb • Debug a honeycomb program	• Understand what a footprint is • Talk about and compare animal footprints • Make their classmate's footprint and compare it with another classmate's and an animal's	• Identify that spiders and insects have a different number of legs • Identify the spider's problem • Think from a different point of reference • Plan and design improvements for the waterspout • Count and group spiders and insects
Unit 6 Why is food important? page 48	• Group items according to their use • Learn how different kinds of soap can make them feel • Experiment on how different brands of soap can clean their hands • Learn about the importance of washing their hands before eating	• Learn about fruit oxidation • Do an experiment with fruits and record its progress • Learn about right and left and play a coder game	• Use play dough to make fruit • Classify food containers according to what they can store, liquids or non-liquids • Analyze food containers to store ravioli in a freezer and think of ways to transform a bottle into a ravioli container	• Check statements about food • Get introduced to the concept of conditional for running a program • Categorize food items into hot and cold • Learn to think of and test hypotheses by answering it questions
Unit 7 How can farm animals help us? page 56	• Learn about the life cycle of a chicken and make a craft • Compare shapes and sizes to a chick's body • Decipher a code to make part of a robot chick	• Identify farm animals and their houses • Design, plan, and build a chicken coop • Learn to calculate how many items are missing in a group	• Group farm animals • Make a graph and compare the number of animals in a farm • Make a sheep mask	• Learn about estimation • Find out what animal products can help them • Learn about texture and make a colorful sheep
Unit 8 Who lives and works in my town? page 64	• Work on spatial concepts and the concept of urban planning • Make a neighborhood model	• Learn about magnetism by making a train move • Develop a program with an algorithm for a railway involving branching (decisions) • Measure and compare the width of a train and railways	• Learn about the things they do at different places in a town • Reflect on essential parts of a house • Make the roof of a house and decorate its garden	• Learn more about the work of firefighters • Make a fire truck ladder and think of ways to improve it • Measure the height of ladders and choose the ladder to save a cat

Presentation

Let's learn about... is a bilingual program that aims to develop a wide variety of skills and subjects. To this end, several additional components ensure that students work on creative learning, pre-coding skills, STEAM lessons, personal, social, and emotional development and much more. Teachers can find a complete mapping of the components online and suggested weekly planning to help them with their lessons in order to make the most of the cross-curricular proposal. All of the components of the program provide students with the opportunity to build a solid foundation and get ready for the challenges ahead.

As part of the ***Let's learn about... Bilingual Program***, the STEAM component aims to encourage students to gather ideas and explore possibilities in order to solve problems and build knowledge from them – and language is the means by which this happens. The acronym STEAM is used to refer to skills related to five learning subjects: Science, Technology, Engineering, Arts, and Math. STEAM skills are mostly developed through hands-on activities that require students to think critically, investigate, make discoveries by trial and error, and reflect on ways to broaden the possibilities of the application of new knowledge.

Learning principles behind STEAM in *Let's learn about...*

The STEAM component in ***Let's learn about... Bilingual Program*** was developed based on the following learning principles:

- Children engage in practical problem-solving from a very early age and they are naturally motivated to do so.
- Children's understanding of the world cannot be imposed; the way they relate the experiences they go through to reality will help them develop their own understanding of the world. Nevertheless, they should be guided in order to find answers and discover new things.
- Although applying certain concepts and skills may seem too challenging for most preschoolers, they are generally capable of developing an understanding of early scientific skills; for instance, if they are provided with visual aid, relatable experiences, and hands-on tasks.
- All STEAM subjects are somehow already part of a child's daily routine: they may identify amounts and shapes in objects or understand that a ball rolls when they kick it, for example.
- Providing preschoolers with meaningful opportunities to develop creative and collaborative work is closely related to how much they may progress in developmental domains and school readiness.
- Students play a leading role in guiding lessons, selecting and reflecting on possible materials they need for a given project, and reflecting on improvements. Although possible outcomes are provided for all tasks involving creating something new, they should be open-ended and support students so that they can cultivate innovative ideas.
- The fundamentals of a lesson include: asking students questions to have them reflect on a problem, plan and create solutions to it, observe and analyze the outcome of this solution and reflect on possible ways to improve it.

What a STEAM lesson involves

As in any other ***Let's learn about...*** component, STEAM lessons propose the establishment of a routine when it comes to the beginning and end of a class, such as greeting their teacher, puppet, and classmates, talking about the schedule for the day, and saying goodbye.

The other activities that are part of a lesson aim not only to present a concept to students, but more importantly, they work towards having students perceive an idea through experimenting. All STEAM subjects explicitly covered in a lesson are displayed at its opening page and in each of the proposed activities. Although subjects are presented separately in each of the activities, all these stages integrate in order to provide opportunities for accomplishing the goals of a lesson.

About the subjects in STEAM

- **Science** – Students are encouraged to make use of the scientific method to experiment and make discoveries about the world. This means that science activities require students to think and create hypotheses before carrying out experiments and evaluating their results.
- **Technology** – Rather than using technological devices as the main tool for technology activities, the program provides an understanding of several man-made objects and basic concepts children should learn in order to understand some fundamental principles of technology, such as common terms, processes, and sequences in programming or dealing with digital tools.
- **Engineering** – When students are invited to build something after analyzing a problem, thinking of the needs, planning and designing a possible solution, they are actually going through steps which are very similar to those an engineer goes through in order to develop a product. The STEAM component also proposes that students analyze their production and think of ways to improve it.

- **Arts –** STEAM is strongly related to thinking critically and creating. When creating something, artistic skills such as painting, drawing, and assembling something in a creative way are necessary. As well as using art as the means to accomplish a goal, students go beyond and explore ways to solve a problem creatively.
- **Math –** This STEAM subject is so present in a child's life that the simple understanding of the space they have available on their desks or tables to put their school material is in fact a math concept they needed to develop. A few other essential concepts that are learned from a very early age are the understanding of sequences, patterns, problem solving, estimating size and weight, and measuring using non-standard tools.

The purposeful integration of these five learning subjects in the lessons aims to promote a wider range of learning opportunities to preschoolers. **Let's learn about…** students should be prepared to combine innovation with taking risks after careful analysis of possible outcomes and engage in experiential learning through problem solving and collaboration.

 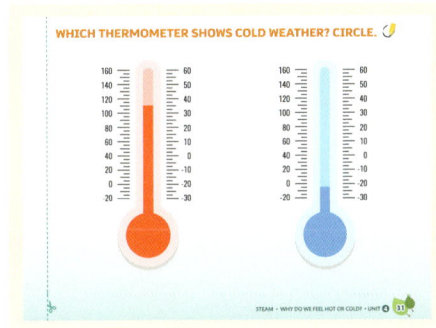

How to work with the STEAM Project Book

All **Let's learn about…** Project Books may have their pages removed. Before starting an activity in their Project Books, students can be instructed to take out the page they are going to work on and add it to a folder of their choice, so that students' work can be shared with parents regularly. This page, together with the projects students have developed in other project lessons, can become part of a portfolio created alongside with the teacher.

The aim of a portfolio is to show the cumulative efforts and progress students have made over time. This is also a great way to evaluate their improvement in all learning areas and the mastery of several skills. Students should be encouraged to share the work in their portfolio with their parents so that they can support their child's learning and be an active part of their development as a student.

An assessment chart is available in the Extra Resources folder at Pearson English Portal for teachers to print and fill out with students' performance and attached to the portfolio folder.

Components

For teachers
- STEAM Teacher's Guide
- Audio library with songs available at Pearson English Portal

For students
- STEAM Project Book with pages that may be removed

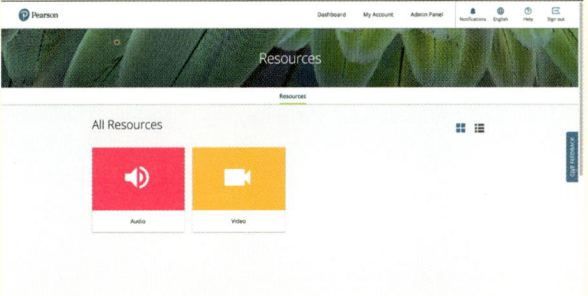

Presentation 7

Unit 1 What do you like about yourself?

Learning goals
- Talk about what germs are and how to avoid spreading them
- Follow a sequence in a story
- Group items according to shape and size
- Use soap to make drawings on black paper

STEAM subjects
- Science
- Technology
- Arts
- Math

Thinking skills
Conceptualizing, applying, analyzing, creating, evaluating

Main language content
Wash your hands. Don't spread germs.
These are germs. My germs are round.
Hygiene: *germs, restroom, soap, toilet, water*

OPENING

Circle time

Materials and preparation
- A bell
- Visual schedule pictures
- Washing facilities (or a bucket with water and pieces of cloth)

Invite students to go to the school washing facilities and wash their hands. Tell them they will learn why they are washing their hands later.
Then have students come back to the classroom and sit in a circle. Have them say *hello*.
Show them all the visual schedule pictures and explain what they are for. Say, *These pictures show our schedule for the day. Let's check it out!* Show all pictures, one at a time, and teach students the name of the subjects. Ask them to say what kinds of things they think they will learn in these subjects and help them understand a little more about them.

> **Note to teachers**
> You can take pictures of the students doing different activities this class: science, technology, engineering, arts, and math activities. Use these pictures for the visual schedule. You can also print out pictures that refer to these activities or other students doing these activities.

Science – What are germs?

Materials and preparation
- Puppet

Talk to the puppet about being clean. If students have already chosen a name in another class, use that name. If not, have students help you choose a name for the puppet.
T: *Hello, (Puppet's name). Do you like to be clean?*
P: *Yes, I wash my hands, I take a shower, and I don't spread germs.*
Ask students if they know what germs are. Ask if they think the word refers to something good or bad. Then say, *Germs are very, very, small living things (organisms) that can cause disease.*

STEAM

Ask, *Is it good to have germs on your hands? How can we get rid of germs?* Allow students to give their opinion freely. Then ask, *Why did we wash our hands before?* And explain that washing their hands is a way of getting rid of germs, so when they shook hands they didn't spread germs to their classmates.

ACTIVE LEARNING

Science – Glitter germs: how do they spread?

Materials and preparation
- Glitter (several colors)
- Soap
- Washing facilities

Tell students that they are going to see today how germs spread very easily although they are invisible to our eyes. Have students stay in a circle. Put a small amount of glitter on the hands of every other student. Say, *Let's shake hands with our classmates!* And invite students to shake hands with the classmate on their right, making sure their classmate's hand gets some glitter, too. When they finish, have them all show their hands. Say, *Look! The glitter is like germs. You touch things, the germs spread.* Ask students how they can avoid this and elicit the phrase *wash our hands*. Take them all to the washing facilities again and have them wash their hands.

> **Note to teachers**
> It is always good to expand the discussion. You can do this by asking questions and having them investigate and think about solutions to the problem of germ-spreading: wash your hands (after coughing or sneezing, before eating), or wash your hands after going to the restroom.

Technology and math – Draw arrows to order the story. Say.

Materials and preparation
- Pencils
- Project Book page 5

Have students open their Project Book to page 5 and look at the pictures. Ask, *Where is the girl here* (pointing to the first picture)? *And here* (pointing to the classroom picture)?
Draw an arrow on the board and tell students that arrows can be used to show what comes next in a story. Invite a few students to draw arrows on the board to show their classmates how to draw. Then have students draw arrows to continue the sequence of the story. Help them understand how the story starts: *First the girl goes to the restroom. Now she is in the toilet stall. Can you see her feet under the door? What comes next?* Elicit that it is the picture of the girl leaving the stall and going to the sink. Continue the sequence with them and remind them to draw the arrows connecting the pictures.
When students finish, help them say what happens in each picture in the correct order.

> **Note to teachers**
> Understanding sequences and how a mistake in sequencing can cause a problem in the final result is a basic coding skill that students can learn from a very early age through different activities, such as putting pictures in order.

DIFFERENTIATED INSTRUCTION

BELOW LEVEL
Science and arts – Soapy drawings

Materials and preparation
- Black construction paper
- Soap bars (one for each student or have them share)

Give each student a bar of soap and a piece of black construction paper. Have them use the soap to draw germs. Ask, *How do you imagine germs are? Let's draw using soap.*
When everyone has finished, organize an exhibit of all the drawings and have students present their work: *These are germs.*

ABOVE LEVEL

Have students do the procedures explained in *Below level*, but after each one presents their germs, have them work in pairs comparing their idea of what germs look like and elicit some ideas: *(Anna's) germs are big. My germs are small. (Anna's) germs have legs. My germs are round.*

CLOSING

Math – Group the germs. Say goodbye.

Materials and preparation
- Students' soap germ drawings

Divide students into two groups. Help them find similarities between their germs and group them. They can identify shapes or size and divide their germs. Then have groups change places and check the other group's germ separation. Encourage students to try to identify how their classmates grouped their germs (by size, by shape, by number?).
When they finish, invite students to help you clean up the classroom and say *goodbye* to them.

> **Note to teachers**
> If possible, send a note to parents asking them to help the students to research possible diseases people can catch when they don't wash their hands before eating. Invite them to tell their classmates about their findings in the following class.

Unit 1 9

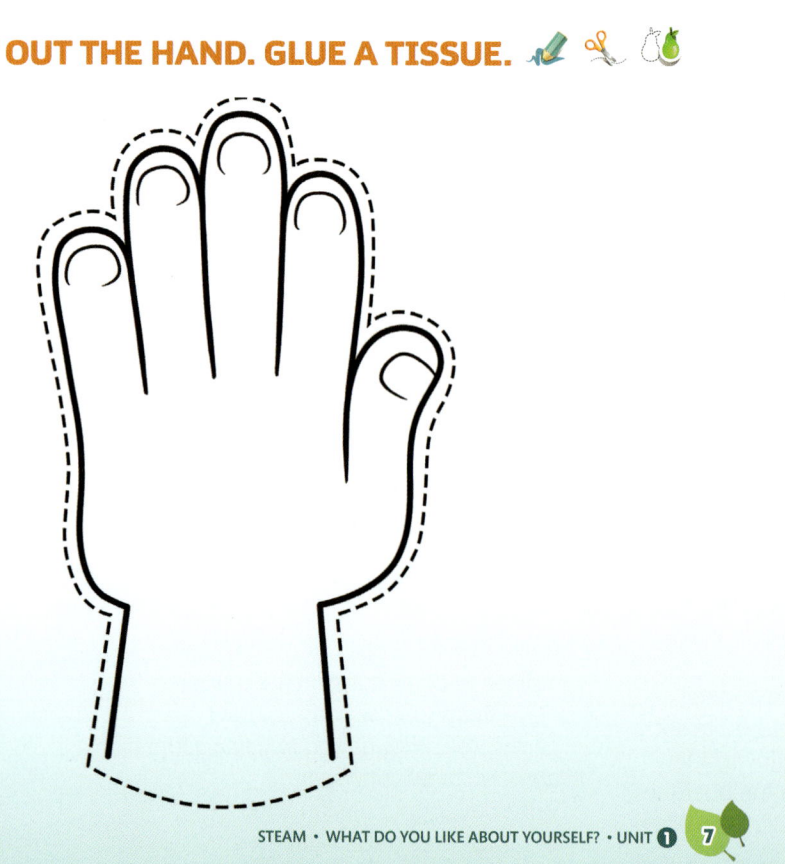

OPENING

Circle time

Materials and preparation
- A bell
- Puppet
- Visual schedule pictures

Say *hello* to students and invite them to sit in a circle. Encourage them to say *hello* to you and the puppet. Make it answer, *Hello, my friends*.
Before the class starts, hide the pictures representing today's schedule and have students look for them. Then place them in the circle.
Teach them an attention-getter to introduce the schedule. Make the bell chime.
T: *Can you hear the chime?*
S: *It's (science) time!*
Show a picture of one of today's activities and elicit, *It's (science) time!* Repeat with the other subjects.

Engineering – The restroom is out of order!

Materials and preparation
- A picture of the staff restroom (or availability and permission to take students there)

Still in a circle, tell students that the restroom they use at school is out of order. Explain that when something is out of order, it needs fixing, so they can't use that restroom for now. Say, *If you need to go to the restroom, you must use the teachers' restroom.*
Take students to the staff restroom or show them a picture of it. Show them the sink, then gesture and say, *Mmm... It's very high! How can you/shorter students wash your/their hands here?* As you take students back to the classroom, start listening to their ideas and continue the discussion in the classroom. Make sure they come up with an idea that can make them step up on something so as to reach the sink.

Learning goals
- Talk about personal hygiene and their face
- Make a cough not/sneeze not model of themselves
- Think of a solution to reach a high sink

STEAM subjects
- Science
- Engineering
- Arts

Thinking skills
Remembering, understanding, applying, analyzing, creating, evaluating

Main language content
It's out of order.
Cover your mouth. You're spreading germs.
Don't spread germs.
Hygiene vocabulary: *cough, germ, sneeze, tissue*
Parts of the face: *eyes, mouth, nose*

Note to teachers
Even though their final product is going to be a stool, make sure to consider all students' ideas and show how great they are. Help them problematize their choices so as to make them reflect and come up with even better ideas.

ACTIVE LEARNING

Engineering – Make a small stool.
Materials and preparation
- Stones, pieces of brick, or pieces of wood
- Two cardboard shoe boxes

Show students a cardboard box and say, *We can use this box to make a stool!* Ask what they think and see if they agree. They might come up with a problem: once you step on the empty box, it will crumple. If they don't, press the box with your hand to show them the problem. Then say, *How can we make this box stronger?* After listening to them, show them the material available to put inside the box.
Help students understand that the stones, bricks, and wood can hold their weight. Have them test. Divide students into two groups and invite them to put the materials into the boxes. Then help a student step onto it and see if it holds their weight. Make sure to be holding the student's hands so as to help and make sure they don't fall or hurt themselves.

Science and arts – Make a cough not/sneeze not model of yourself.
Materials and preparation
- Colored markers
- Glue
- Paper or plastic plates (one per student)
- Play dough
- Puppet
- Sequins
- Stones
- String
- Tissues

Take the puppet and pretend that it is coughing very noisily. Say, *Hey, you're spreading germs! Cover your mouth! Use a tissue or your arm.*
Pretend you're coughing and sneezing and teach students these words. Tell students they are going to make an artwork showing their face and how to cover their mouth when they cough or sneeze. Give them the paper plates and elicit the shape of the plates. Then invite them to brainstorm ideas on how they can transform this plate into a canvas for their facial characteristics. Present the material you have and allow time for students to exchange ideas on how each of the materials can be used. Explain that each of them can make the facial characteristics using whatever material they want. Monitor and help as needed.
When they have finished making the faces, have students place their own hand in front of the paper-plate face every time you say *sneeze not* or *cough not*. You may pretend to be sneezing or coughing before saying the phrases.

DIFFERENTIATED INSTRUCTION

BELOW LEVEL
Science and arts – Color and cut out the hand. Glue a tissue.
Materials and preparation
- Paper tissues or towels (one per student)
- Popsicle sticks (one per student)
- Project Book page 7
- Scissors (age appropriate) or cut out the hand pictures before class
- Students' face artwork
- Tape

First have students open their Project Book to page 7 and color the hand. As they are coloring, help them cut out the hand and put the popsicle stick on it using tape. Then give them a tissue and tell them to glue its top at the back of the hand, as if it were the palm, leaving the rest loose.
After that tell students to take their face artwork and pretend it is sneezing or coughing as you tell them to. Every time you say, for example, *Cough!* they will pretend the face is coughing and raise the hand with tissue in front of the mouth. Repeat a few more times using both words, *cough* and *sneeze*.

ABOVE LEVEL
Have students do the first step described in *Below level*. As their hand holding a tissue is ready, divide them into groups, ask them to take the face artwork they made, and have one student per group say *cough* or *sneeze* for their classmates to raise the hand holding a tissue in front of the mouth that is part of the face artwork. Make sure all students in a group have a chance to give the commands *cough* or *sneeze*.

Note to teachers
As students are still learning the correct scissors grip and how to cut paper, allow them to cut the area around the hand and fingers without cutting in the shape of fingers.

CLOSING

Play *Watch the germs!* Say goodbye.
Materials and preparation
- Four drawings of germs (you can have students draw germs)
- Tape
- Ten pieces of butcher paper or black construction paper

Take students outside or make space in the classroom. Use tape to place the pieces of paper lined up on the floor, two pieces in each line and one in between lines at the end of the lines. Have students close their eyes and place the germ drawings underneath one piece of paper in each line, either all on the right or all on the left. Have students choose one of the two lines of pieces of paper to hop along. Then have them help you check where the germs were and who stepped on the germs. You can play the game again if time allows.
Ask students to help you clean up. Then say *goodbye* to them and have them say *goodbye* to you.

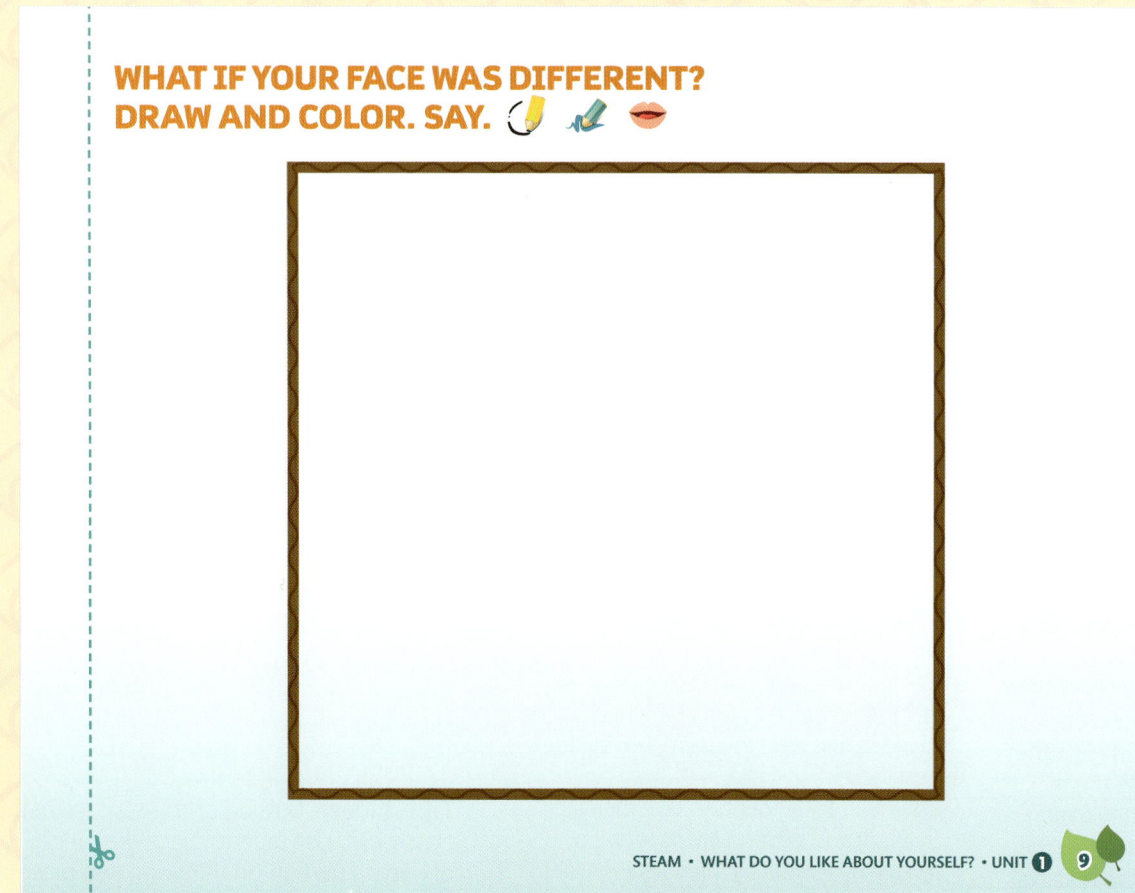

Learning goals
- Talk about hypotheses and hypothetical situations
- Understand that *What if* questions are about possibilities, imagination, and creativity
- Solve problems in a creative and critical way

STEAM subjects
- Science
- Arts
- Math

Thinking skills
Understanding, applying, analyzing, creating

Main language content
What if you had two mouths? Would you walk?
It's difficult to sleep. You can see the sun more.
What time is time to sleep?
Parts of the body: *ears, eyes, feet, hands, mouth, nose*
Colors: *blue, green, red, yellow*
Parts of the day: *day, night*
Numbers: *1-5*

OPENING

Circle time

Materials and preparation
- A bell
- A book
- Puppet
- Visual schedule pictures

Say *hello* to students. Encourage them to say *hello* to you and the puppet. Make it answer, *Hello, my friends*.
Cover the pictures of today's schedule using a book. Hold the pictures behind the book and show part of them only. Ask students if they can guess what activity it is. Repeat with the other picture.
Show one picture at a time, make the bell chime, and ask, *Can you hear the chime?*
Elicit, *It's (arts) time!* Repeat with the other subjects.

Science – What if?

Have students in a circle. Say that they are going to travel now to *Imagination Land* and ask, *What if there were no nights?*
Explain to students that your questions have many possible answers and that they should all feel free to imagine such an answer.
Encourage students to be creative in their answers. Model an answer: *So there are no nights, only day. You cant see the moon!*
Elicit answers such as, *It's difficult to sleep. You can see the sun more. What time is time to sleep?*

ACTIVE LEARNING

Science and arts – What if there was only one color in the world?

Materials and preparation
- Brushes
- One color of paint or crayon
- Scrap paper
- Sequins
- Sheets of paper

Ask students, *What if there was only one color in the world?*
Allow students to imagine the world with one color only. If necessary, use the following questions to elicit discussion: *What would be like? What color would that be? Green? Red? Yellow?*
Give each student a piece of paper and have them choose one color of paint or crayon. Then have them draw a portrait of how the world would be with just one color. Students can add other components to the artwork, but they can't use more than one color.
Collect portraits and organize an exhibit for all students to observe. Ask questions such as, *How would you feel about living in this "all green" world? What would you miss the most?* Let them be critical about these changes and also make hypotheses about life in the world they created.

> **Note to teachers**
> *What if* questions help students learn to analyze possibilities, be creative, and test hypotheses. Hypothesizing is the basis for the process of determining the effects on outcomes, which is the method by which scientists prove theories.

Science, arts, and math – What if your face was different? Draw and color. Say.

Materials and preparation
- Crayons or colored pencils
- Project Book page 9

Ask students, *What if your face was different?* Allow students to imagine human beings with one eye, three noses, and two mouths, for example. Ask, *Would you be sad or happy? Would you eat more with two mouths?*
Have students open their Project Book to page 9. Give them crayons or colored pencils and have them draw themselves with different facial characteristics. Walk around, check students' work, and make hypotheses according to what they are drawing: *Wow! Three eyes? What if we had three eyes?*

DIFFERENTIATED INSTRUCTION

BELOW LEVEL
Science – What if we had no feet?
Divide students into small groups. Ask, *What if you had no feet?* Allow students time to imagine and share ideas of how they would be. If necessary, ask the following questions to elicit ideas: *Would you walk? How would you walk?* Invite groups to demonstrate how they would walk and tell their classmates their ideas.

ABOVE LEVEL
Science – What if we had no…?
Divide students into small groups. Assign each group one of the questions: *What if you had no feet? What if you had no hands? What if you had no ears?* Have them talk to their classmates and think of the situations. Help them if necessary.
Invite groups to demonstrate the possible consequences of their hypotheses without saying what the hypothesis is. Then invite the rest of the class to guess: *What if you had no (hands)?*

> **Note to teachers**
> This activity is also a great way of getting students to think about what the life of a person with a disability might be like and think of ways to make these people's lives easier.

CLOSING

Do a gallery walk. Say goodbye.

Materials and preparation
- Students' portraits
- Tape

Collect students' portraits to place them on the wall and make a gallery walk. Tell students to help you understand the hypothesis created in each portrait. Have them think of possibilities for a few of the hypotheses: *Wow! A hand on our head? What if we had a hand on our head?* Elicit answers.
Then ask students to put away their portraits and say *goodbye* to each other, to you, and to the puppet.

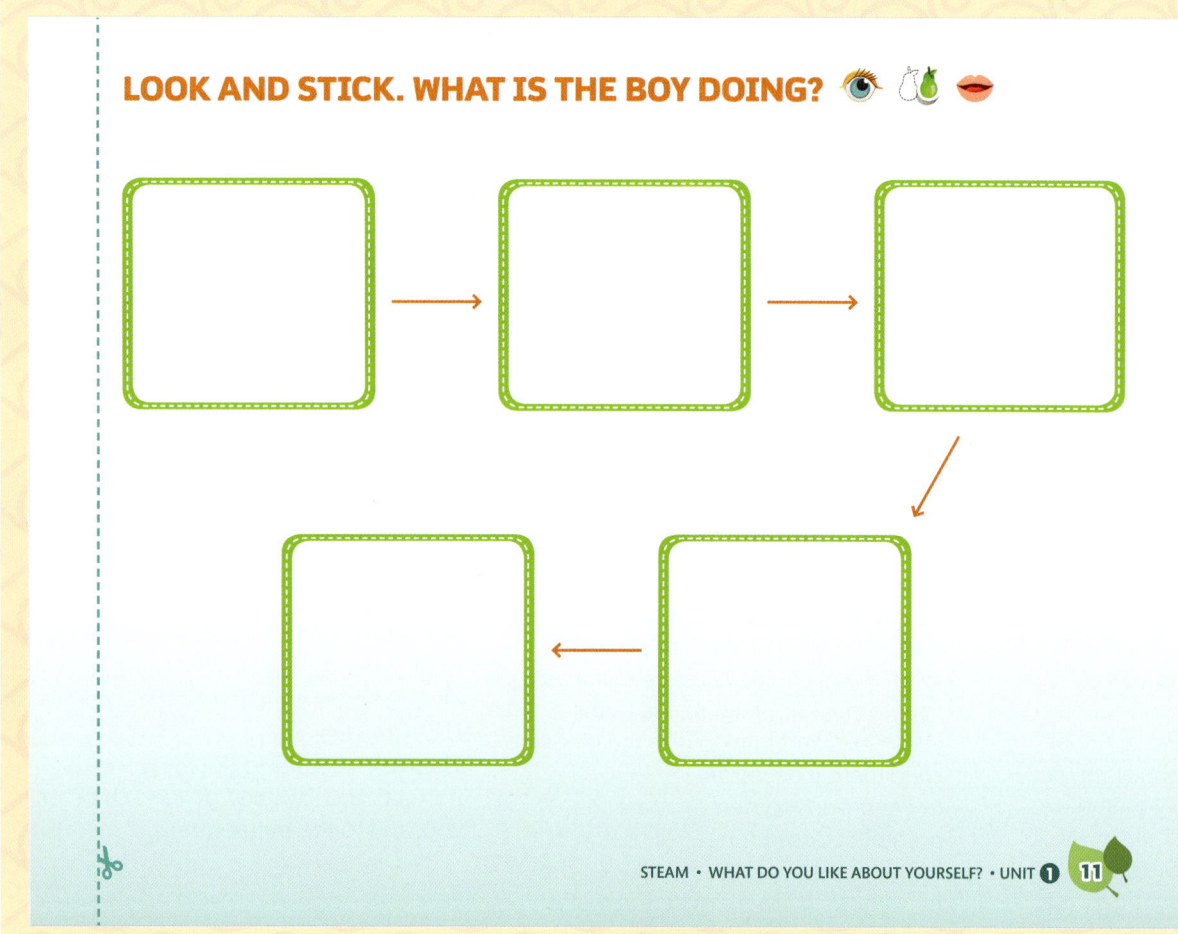

Learning goals
- Talk about their body functions
- Identify the algorithm of a mindfulness exercise
- Learn how to categorize items

STEAM subjects
- Science
- Technology
- Math

Thinking skills
Remembering, understanding, applying, analyzing, creating

Main language content
What can you see?
Breath in, one, two, three.
Parts of the body: *lungs, nose*
Sequencers: *after, before*
Mindfulness exercises: *breathe in, breathe out, yoga*

OPENING

Circle time
Materials and preparation
- A bell
- Puppet
- Visual schedule pictures

Say *hello* to students. Encourage them to say *hello* to you and the puppet. Make it answer, *Hello, my friends*.
Hide the pictures representing today's schedule and have students look for them. Then have students sit in a circle and place the pictures in the circle. Make the bell chime and say, *Can you hear the chime?*
Show a picture of one of today's activities and elicit, *It's (technology) time!* Repeat with the other subjects.

Play *Blow, blow, blow the pompoms.*
Materials and preparation
- Chalk or masking tape
- Pompoms
- Straws

Take students outside or make space in the classroom. Use the masking tape or the chalk to mark a starting line and a finish line on the floor for a pompom race. Give each student a straw and a pompom and have them blow their pompoms to the finish line. Explain to students that they were able to make their pompoms move using air that comes from their lungs. Ask, *Where are our lungs?* Help students identify where the lungs are. Say that they have two lungs that help them breathe. Have them breathe in and out with their hands over their chest to feel the lungs filling up with air.
Ask them if they felt their body fill with air and if they could imagine their lungs full of air. You can invite a few students to draw on the board (or on the floor, if you are outside) the way they imagine their lungs filled with air look like.

Note to teachers

Having students breathe in and out and making them aware of the way they breathe helps them understand what their breath can say about the way they feel. It is a good way to introduce how the respiratory system works.

ACTIVE LEARNING

Science – Mindfulness exercise

Have students sit in a very comfortable corner of the classroom or outside in the schoolyard and tell them they will do a breathing exercise with you.
Say, *Breathe in, one, two, three. Breathe out, one two, three.* Invite a few students to also give the breathing instructions.

Science and technology – Look and stick. What is the boy doing?

Materials and preparation

- Project Book page 11
- Unit 1 Stickers

Have students open their Project Book to page 11. Then direct them to the stickers at the end of their Project Book and invite them to look at the pictures. Ask, *What can you see? What is the boy doing in the scenes?* (yoga, breathing, blowing up a balloon).
Elicit that breathing is pulling air into our body – breathe in as you say this – and then letting it out – breathe out as you say this. Tell them to think which scene comes first. In pairs, have them order the next four scenes. Check their answers before they stick the pictures on the page. Have them copy the boy's actions and help you say the steps.

Note to teachers

An algorithm is a set of rules to be followed in order to solve a problem. The problem presented here is to learn to breathe correctly in order to learn about mindfulness. You can tell students that, in order to complete a task, there is a list of steps we need to follow. If we can follow these steps, we can accomplish the expected result.

DIFFERENTIATED INSTRUCTION

BELOW LEVEL
Science – Breathing with a balloon

Materials and preparation

- Balloons (one per student)

Tell students to breathe in and breathe out. After breathing out, say, *Breathe out again, and again*. Students will show some difficulty doing this as they have already let the air out. Ask, *What do we need to do before we breathe out?* If necessary, breathe in to help them remember. Remind students that this sequence is important for the breathing exercise to work well.

Then give students a balloon and have them copy the boy breathing in and out blowing up the balloon. Tell them to watch their classmates, too. Say, *This balloon is like a lung. Do you remember the lung?* Point to your chest. Have students breathe in and out and check how their balloon fills with air.

ABOVE LEVEL

Tell students to breathe in and breathe out. After breathing out, say, *Breathe out again, and again*. Students will show some difficulty doing this as they have already let the air out. Keep saying that until someone says something or you see someone breathing in. If someone breathes in before breathing out, say, *Look! (Student's name) isn't breathing out. What is he/she doing?* Elicit *breathing in* and ask why. Make sure students understand that breathing out is what comes after breathing in in the mindfulness exercise.
Ask students if this sequence is important for the exercise and elicit reasons.
Then give students a balloon and have them copy the boy breathing in and out blowing the balloon. Tell them to watch their classmates, too. Ask, *What part of our body inflates when we breathe in?* Elicit answers. Point to your chest to remind students of the lungs, if needed.

CLOSING

Talk about the air you breathe. Say goodbye.

Materials and preparation

- Students' balloons from previous activity

Have students blow up their balloon. Ask, *What is air? Can you see air? What color is it?* Make sure students understand that they can't see the air.
Divide them into pairs and have them let the air out of their balloon next to their classmate's hand. Ask, *Can you feel the air? Is it hot? Is it cold?* Allow students to share with everyone their sensation with the air blowing on their hands. Help them understand that, even though they can't see the air, it exists and it can be felt. After that, allow students to use their balloons to wave goodbye to you and the puppet. Say *goodbye* to them.

Unit 2 Why do we go to school?

Learning goals
- Develop balance, body control, concentration, and posture through dancing
- Categorize garbage cans by color
- Categorize waste as compost or recyclable
- Make recycled paper

STEAM subjects
- Science
- Arts
- Math

Thinking skills
Conceptualizing, applying, analyzing, evaluating

Main language content
Green bin! Yellow bin!
What can we recycle?
It's recyclable. It's compost.
Numbers: *1-12*
Colors: *green, yellow*
Garbage: *banana peel, bottle cap, chicken bone, orange peel, paper, plastic bottle, plastic cup*

OPENING

Circle time
Materials and preparation
- A bell
- Puppet
- Visual schedule pictures

Bring out the puppet and start by having it greet the students. After they greet the puppet, have the puppet greet you, too. Then elicit *Hello!* and ask students how they are today. Show them how to respond using their thumbs.
Hide the pictures representing today's schedule and have students look for them. Ask those who found the pictures to say what they will learn today. Help if needed.
Make the bell chime and ask, *Can you hear the chime?* Show a picture of one of today's activities and elicit, *It's (math) time!* Repeat with the other subjects.

Arts – Balloon dance
Materials and preparation
- Balloons (one per student)
- Classical music

Before class, blow the balloons and let them float around the classroom. Play classical music and invite students to dance to it while playing gently with one of the balloons. Explain that their dance and play with the balloon needs to be gentle, just like the music they are listening to.

ACTIVE LEARNING

Science – Make recycled paper.

Materials and preparation
- Banana peel
- Plastic containers to soak paper
- Shredded scrap paper (you can divide them by color)
- Water

Show students the banana peel and shreds of scrap paper. Ask, *Can I put these two in the same bin? Why (not)? Are they different?* As students answer, present the words *compost* and *recyclable* and say that this is how we call two types of waste.

Explain that compost is what comes from plants and animals, like leaves, grass, fruit, and vegetable scraps, and recyclable waste is all from man-made materials, such as steel and aluminum cans, glass bottles, cardboard boxes, newspapers, and plastic bottles. These items can be recycled and become new products. Explain to students that you are going to make recycled paper together.

With students' help shred the paper into small pieces, put them in some plastic containers, and cover them with water. Let them soak overnight. Explain to them that to make recycled paper they need to leave the paper in water for one day. Invite them to watch the paper as it is now to compare it with the way it will be the next day.

> **Note to teachers**
> This project will take up two classes since some parts of the activity need to be prepared and left overnight to dry.

Science and math – Play the recycling game. Color the items green or yellow.

Materials and preparation
- Colored pencils
- Project Book page 13

Have students open their Project Book to page 13. Draw their attention to the two bins. Explain that the yellow bin is for compost and the green bin is for recyclable materials. Elicit some examples of compost and recyclable materials. Then elicit the names of the items next to the bins. Tell students they are going to play the recycling game. Invite a few students to call out an item, one student at a time, and have the others say *green bin* or *yellow bin*. Tell them the correct answer and say that only those who have chosen the correct bin color get to color the picture. After having worked with all items, have students count how many items they have colored. After the game, have students work in pairs to color the items they missed in the game.

DIFFERENTIATED INSTRUCTION

BELOW LEVEL
Science and math – Green or yellow bin?

Materials and preparation
- Project Book page 13

Divide students into pairs. Have a student cover the items of Project Book page 13 with their book or a pencil case. Tell this student to say a bin color, for example, *green bin*, and have their classmate say one item that goes in that bin. They can check answers by uncovering the pictures.
Have them play a few more times taking turns.

ABOVE LEVEL

Divide students into pairs. Have a student cover the items of Project Book page 13 with their book or a pencil case. Tell this student to say a bin color, for example, *green bin*, and have their classmate say as many items as they can that go in that bin.

They can check answers by uncovering the pictures. Have them compare how many correct items each of them got.

CLOSING

Arts and math – The compost and recyclable items dance

Materials and preparation
- Audio library – songs
- Copies of the items on Project Book page 13 (one item per student)

Give each student a picture of an item. Have them tell each other what they have and if it is compost or recyclable. Then play their favorite song and tell them that they will sing and dance. During the song shout, for example, *Recyclable waste, freeze!* and have all students who have a recyclable item freeze until you say *recyclable waste, dance!* Take turns between the two types of waste.
Then play the song again and have students wave goodbye to you and the puppet. Wave to them, too.

> **Note to teachers**
> Send a note to parents asking students to bring a few recyclable materials to make a toy. Send suggestions, too: plastic bottles, medication boxes, buttons (not too small), aluminum cans, bottle caps, plastic cups.

WHICH ITEMS ARE MADE FROM RECYCLABLE MATERIALS? CIRCLE.

STEAM • WHY DO WE GO TO SCHOOL? • UNIT 2 — 15

Learning goals
- Understand why recycling is important
- Design recycled toys
- Make color patterns out of recyclable paper

STEAM subjects
- Science
- Engineering
- Arts
- Math

Thinking skills
Remembering, understanding, applying, analyzing, creating, evaluating

Main language content
What can we recycle?
What is the pattern?
Recyclable waste: *glass, metal, paper, plastic*
Colors: *blue, green, orange, red, yellow*
Toys and school materials: *pencil case, swing, toy car*

OPENING

Circle time

Materials and preparation
- A bell
- A book
- Puppet
- Visual schedule pictures

Say *hello* to students. Encourage them to say *hello* to you and the puppet. Make it answer, *Hello, my friends*. Then invite students to sit in a circle.
Cover the pictures of today's schedule using a book. Hold the pictures behind the book and show part of them only. Ask students if they can guess what activity it is. Repeat with the other pictures. Show one picture at a time, make the bell chime, and ask, *Can you hear the chime?*
Elicit, *It's (engineering) time!* Repeat with the other subjects.

Science – Why do we recycle?

Materials and preparation
- A notebook made out of recyclable paper (optional)

Go over the concept of recycling with students. Ask, *What is recycling? Why do we recycle?* And allow them to give their opinion or make guesses. If you have a notebook or any other material made out of recyclable paper, show it to students and encourage them to compare it with one that wasn't made out of recyclable paper: *What color is the paper here? And here? Can I write here? And here? Can I draw?* Make sure students understand that both types of paper can work for the same purposes, they just look different.
Explain that we recycle for two reasons. First, because it is good for the Earth and second, because we save up space in our landfills – the places where most trash is sent to after collection. Ask, *What kind of things can we recycle?* (Plastic, glass, metal, paper)

> **Note to teachers**
> Having some visual aids when talking about new concepts is extremely important for young learners, so whenever possible

 STEAM

bring materials that can help them understand the topic of a lesson.

ACTIVE LEARNING

Science and arts – Recycled handmade paper

Materials and preparation
- A frame with mesh stretched and nailed over it
- Blender
- Containers with water and paper from previous class
- Cookie cutters
- Dried flowers (optional)
- Food coloring and glitter (optional)
- Large container that can fit the frame for the water to run
- Water

Explain to students that now it's time to go back to your recycled paper, which you started producing in the previous class. Put the soaked paper in the blender and mix it until you get a smooth texture. Add water as necessary. Remind students that the blender can only be used by you and that it can be quite dangerous to use it without adult supervision.
Divide students into small groups. Divide the paper mixture into small portions and add glitter, leaves, and/or food coloring to them. Have each group decide what they want to add to their pulp.
Place the cookie cutters on the frame with the mesh pour the pulp into the cookie cutters and make sure it spreads evenly. Press the pulp against the frame to allow excess water to drip away.
Let the pulp dry and gently peel it off the net, picking up the cookie cutter.
Next choose one of the projects to do with students.

> **Note to teachers**
> So as to allow the paper to dry, you can start your class with this activity and then talk about recycling with students. Sometimes the paper can take longer to dry, so you can bring a few models ready to show students the rest of the process.

Science, arts, and math – Making patterns out of recyclable paper

Materials and preparation
- Brushes
- Paint
- Paper made in previous activity

Have students make different shapes using the pulp. Ask them what shapes they can think of and have them make about six of them. Then divide students into small groups and assign each group a color pattern, for example, *Red, blue, red, blue*. Have them make colored stripes on the paper according to the pattern assigned. Then have everyone walk around checking the patterns made by their classmates. Ask, *What is the pattern here? What colors repeat? Yellow, green, yellow,...?* Elicit the patterns from students.

Science and math – Which items are made from recyclable materials? Circle.

Materials and preparation
- Pencils
- Project Book page 15

Have students open their Project Book to page 15. Ask, *What can you see?* Elicit the words *pencil case, (toy) car,* and *swing*. *What is different about some of the things in the pictures?* Have students circle the items that are made from recyclable materials. Point to both swings and ask, *Can I play in this swing? Is it fun? What about this swing? Is it fun, too?*

DIFFERENTIATED INSTRUCTION

BELOW LEVEL
Engineering and arts – Make a toy from recyclable materials.

Materials and preparation
- Hot glue (teacher use only)
- Masking tape
- Students' recyclable materials

Have students work in groups and take the recyclable materials they brought from home. Tell them to share materials and think of toys they can make together from the materials they have brought. Allow them to plan first and remind them to listen to their classmates' ideas. Monitor their planning and help them come up with solutions as needed. Then have students design their toys by putting recyclable materials together. If they need hot glue, have them take the materials to you, explain how to put the parts together and hold them for you to use the glue.

ABOVE LEVEL
Have students do the same steps explained in *Below level*, but after they have finished making their toys, have groups analyze the work of other groups and give students tips on how to improve it.

CLOSING

Make a recyclable toy exhibit. Say goodbye.

Materials and preparation
- Name tags
- Students' craft toys
- Tape

Have students help you set up an exhibit with the toys they made somewhere in the school, where other students can see them. Have them name their toys, write the name on a sheet of paper and invite students to write their names underneath. Place the name tags next to their work and invite students from other classes to visit the exhibit.
When the exhibit is over, take students back to the classroom and say *bye* or *goodbye* to them.

> **Note to teachers**
> If students can't write their names yet, invite them to write the initial letter of their name and write the rest of the name yourself.

COUNT AND COLOR THE CIRCLES ON EACH MUSICAL INSTRUMENT.

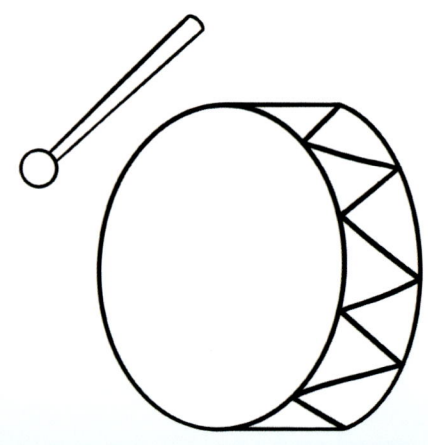
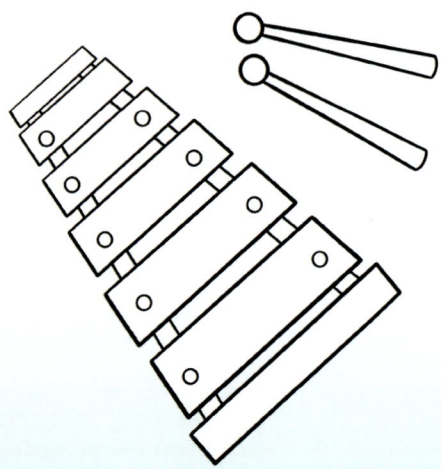

STEAM • WHY DO WE GO TO SCHOOL? • UNIT 2 • 17

Learning goals
- Learn about sounds, music, and rhythm
- Measure different amounts of water
- Think of ways to make a musical instrument collage using shapes

STEAM subjects
- Science
- Engineering
- Arts
- Math

Thinking skills
Remembering, understanding, applying, analyzing, creating

Main language content
Is it the same? Is it different?
Musical instruments: *drums, electric guitar, piano, xylophone*
Colors: *blue, green, orange, purple, red, yellow*
Shapes: *circle, rectangle, square, triangle*
Numbers: *1-10*

OPENING

Circle time
Materials and preparation
- A bell
- A book
- Puppet
- Visual schedule pictures

Say *hello* to students. Encourage them to say *hello* to you and the puppet. Make it answer, *Hello, my friends*. Then invite students to sit in a circle.
Cover the pictures of today's schedule using a book. Hold the pictures behind the book and show part of them only. Ask students if they can guess what activity it is. Repeat with the other pictures.
Show one picture at a time, make the bell chime, and ask, *Can you hear the chime?*
Elicit, *It's (arts) time!* Repeat with the other subjects.

Arts – Copy the rhythm.
Materials and preparation
- Audio library – songs
- Two pencils per student

Ask students if they like it when there is music in class. Ask, *Can you remember any songs?* And have students sing if they remember any songs.
Make a beat using two pencils and have students join in with pencils, too. Help them copy the rhythm. Play the *Hello song* (track 02) or any other song they like and make a new beat using two pencils. When the song ends, invite one or two students to create a new beat for their classmates to copy. Remind them that they don't need to use the pencils. They can clap, blow air, etc., but they must follow a pattern, such as clapping twice and blowing once, clapping twice and blowing once.

STEAM

ACTIVE LEARNING

Science and arts – Make a xylophone.

Materials and preparation
- Cup
- Five glasses (or glass jars) of the same size
- Food coloring (three colors to mix)
- Pictures of the following instruments: drums, piano, triangle, xylophone
- Water

Tell students that today they are going to make a xylophone, which is a percussion instrument. Ask, *Does anyone know what this means? A percussion instrument is any object that produces sound when struck.* Ask if they can think of other examples of percussion instruments. Display the pictures of the other percussion instruments and show them to students. Teach them the words.

Now explain that in order to make the xylophone, you are going to put the glasses one next to the other and fill each one with a different amount of water. Ask for students' help to measure one cup of water and pour it into the first glass. For the second glass, pour 4/5 of a cup of water, for the third 3/5 of a cup of water, and so on. Decrease the amount of water by 1/5 in each glass.

Invite students to color the water in each glass with a different color using food coloring. Have them mix two colors to see what color comes out.

> **Note to teachers**
> This is a good moment to show students how to divide the glass/jar into five equal parts. You can use a tape for that. Put pieces of tape around the jar leaving the same distance between one another.

Science and arts – Play the instrument.

Materials and preparation
- Metal spoon
- Pen
- Pencil
- Plastic spoon

Gather students around a table, put the glasses from the previous activity in the middle. Then use a pencil to tap each of the glasses, and ask them why they think each glass makes a different sound. Elicit a few hypotheses from the students. Students should notice that the glass filled with the most water made sounds in the lowest pitch while the glass with the least amount of water in it made sounds in the highest pitch. However, they won't be able to explain why. So tell them that the sound changes a little depending on how much water there is in the glass.

Have students try tapping the glasses with different materials such as a pencil, a metal spoon, a pen, their fingernails, or a plastic spoon. At this point they should notice slight differences in the pitch when tapping the glasses using different materials.

Math – Count and color the circles on each musical instrument.

Materials and preparation
- Colored pencils
- Project Book page 17

Have students open their Project Book to page 17. Ask them to name the musical instruments they can identify. Then ask, *Can you find any circles on the musical instruments?* Have them identify the circle on the drum, the small circles on the drum stick, and the circles on the xylophone. Then work with the other shapes, too. Have students choose a color for the circles they find on the musical instruments.
When they finish, ask them to count how many circles they could find.

> **Note to teachers**
> Encouraging students to identify shapes on objects is a great way to help them develop their logical and analytic thinking.

DIFFERENTIATED INSTRUCTION

BELOW LEVEL
Engineering, arts, and math – Make an electric guitar out of shapes.

Materials and preparation
- Colored paper triangles, big and small ones, and rectangles (when glued together they can form a guitar)
- Glue
- Pencils
- Picture of a guitar
- Sheets of paper

Divide students into pairs. Give each pair two rectangles and two triangles. Ask, *How can you make an electric guitar using these shapes?* Have students talk to each other and think of ways to put the shapes together and form an electric guitar.
When they have figured it out, check their ideas and invite them to glue the guitar on a piece of paper.

ABOVE LEVEL

Have students do the same steps explained in *Below level*, but after they finish, ask them to think of ways they can make their guitar better. Listen to their ideas and allow them to test a few of them using an erasable pencil. Then say, *How can you make it better using a small triangle?* Help students understand that they can make the head of the guitar with a small triangle.

CLOSING

Sing the *Goodbye song* and make a beat.

Materials and preparation
- Pencils or sticks

Ask students if they can remember the lyrics of the *Goodbye song*. Help them sing. Then divide students into small groups and have each group suggest a beat to play for the others to sing the song. Give them sticks and have them play by tapping their tables. Have all groups suggest a beat. Then say *goodbye* to all students and elicit *goodbye*.

IDENTIFY THE BUGS IN THIS SCHOOL ROUTINE. CROSS THEM OUT. 👁 ✗

START

  FINISH

STEAM • WHY DO WE GO TO SCHOOL? • UNIT 2 • 19

Learning goals
- Talk about school routines
- Spot and debug a problem in a program
- Identify the sequence in their school routine
- Make a school routine poster and display it in the classroom

STEAM subjects
- Technology
- Arts
- Math

Thinking skills
Remembering, understanding, applying, analyzing, creating

Main language content
What is your favorite school routine?
It's school routine. It's not school routine.
Bug. Debug.
School routine: *circle time, learning centers, play time, poster, routine, snack time, story time*

OPENING

Circle time

Materials and preparation
- A bell
- Puppet
- Visual schedule pictures

Greet students and have them greet you back. Ask, *How are you?* and have students answer.
Have them sit in a circle. Place the visual schedule pictures face down in the circle. Have two students turn them over and say what activity they represent. Make the bell chime and say, *Can you hear the chime?*
Show a picture of one of today's activities and elicit, *It's (technology) time!* Repeat with the other subjects.

Arts – School routine mime

Still sitting in a circle, whisper a moment of the students' usual schedule to a student and have them mime it, for example, *story time*. Invite the other students to guess what it is. Have different students play. Also invite a few students to think of a moment of the class themselves and mime for the rest of the class.

 22 STEAM

ACTIVE LEARNING

Arts and math – Our daily routine

Materials and preparation
- Clothing pin
- Crayons
- Glitter and/or sequins
- Glue
- Camera (if available)
- Pictures of students doing different activities or copies of the visual pictures schedule
- Poster or butcher paper
- Scissors

Go over the daily routine with the class. Ask, *What is the first thing we do in class in the morning? What do we do next?* Elicit the words *story (time), snack, play, circle.*

Tell students you are going to make a school routine poster and you will need their help to make it beautiful.

If you have a camera available, divide students into groups and assign each group one activity from the daily routine. Take pictures of them. If not, make copies of the visual schedule.

With students' help, choose the pictures that are show the at school and order them. If there is an activity that is not there, encourage students to make a drawing of it and add it to the poster in the right order.

> **Note to teachers**
> The order of activities might vary according to the organization of the class. However, the aim here is that students can think of a chronological order for the activities, such as having circle time at the beginning and saying goodbye at the end of the class.

Technology – Identify the bugs in this school routine. Cross them out.

Materials and preparation
- Project Book page 19

Have students open their Project Book to page 19 and explain that there are bugs in the school routine. Ask, *What is a bug in computer language? Is a bug an animal only?* Help students understand that when they are playing a game or using any other program in a computer or tablet, for example, and it stops working because of a problem, we call this problem a bug. Ask students to spot the "bug" in the sequence and cross it out. Say, *Let's find something that is not in the correct place.* Elicit answers as a class. Make sure students can identify that the boy putting his pajamas on, the child in the bathtub, and the child watching TV are not part of the school routine.

> **Note to teachers**
> Debugging means spotting and fixing problems in a program. Students can understand the basic concept related to it when looking for problems in a sequence that prevents it from reaching its expected aim.

DIFFERENTIATED INSTRUCTION

BELOW LEVEL
Math – Roll the dice and say the routine.

Materials and preparation
- Tokens (one per student)
- Two dice per group

Rote count to twelve. Then help students roll the dice a few times and count how many dots there are on both dice. Divide them into small groups. Have them roll the dice and count the dots. Then have them move their token that number of houses forward and say what they can see, *school routine* or *not school routine*. Make sure all students have a turn.

> **Note to teachers**
> You can use coins, crayons, or any other small object as tokens for games. This way you also encourage students to be creative when choosing a token.

ABOVE LEVEL

Divide students into small groups. Roll the dice once to show them how to count the dots. Have them roll the dice and count how many dots there are on both dice. Then have them move their token that number of houses forward and say what they can see: *circle time, singing, story time, watching TV*. Make sure all students have a turn.

> As you monitor the activity, ask a few students, *Is (watching TV) part of the school routine? Is (circle time) part of the school routine?*

CLOSING

Talk about your favorite moment in the schedule. Say goodbye.

Ask students what it is they love about school. Ask, *Is it your classmates? The teacher? The activities?*
After that, wave goodbye to students and have them say *goodbye* to you.

Unit 3 How can you help your family at home?

DRAW ARROWS TO ORDER THE STORY.

Learning goals
- Talk about movies
- Understand the logical order in a story through pictures
- Learn that old movies were silent
- Make a stop motion animation

STEAM subjects
- Technology
- Arts
- Math

Thinking skills
Conceptualizing, applying, analyzing, creating, evaluating

Main language content
What is your favorite movie?
I like this movie. It's a silent movie.
They're in the car. They're having ice cream.
Family: *brother, dad, mom, sister*
Chores: *sweep the floor, take out the garbage, wash the dishes*

OPENING

Circle time

Materials and preparation
- A bell
- Visual schedule pictures

Have all the students sit in a circle. Greet them and invite them to greet you back. Review the procedures for gathering in a circle. Hide the pictures representing today's schedule and have students look for them. Then place them in the circle. Use the attention-getter to introduce today's schedule. Make the bell chime and ask, *Can you hear the chime?* Ask students if they remember how to reply and help as needed.
Show a picture of one of today's activities and elicit, *It's (math) time!* Repeat with the other subjects.

Arts – Movie talk

Materials and preparation
- A soft ball
- Several DVDs and/or posters of children's movies (optional)

As students are sitting in the circle, discuss with them the following:
What is your favorite movie?
What movies do you like to watch?
What movies have you seen? Have you ever seen a 3D movie? How is it different from a 2D movie?
Toss the ball to a student and allow them to say a little about the movies they have watched. Remind them to only speak when they are holding the ball and help them understand when it is time to toss the ball to someone else.

ACTIVE LEARNING

Technology and arts – My family stop-motion animation

Materials and preparation
- Background
- Copies of the family members flashcards
- Paint
- Projector and a stop-motion animation movie (optional) or three copies of pictures showing the sequence of a story in a stop-motion animated movie
- Smartphone (if available)
- Stop motion animation app (there are many free versions online) (if available)
- Tripod or stand to hold your device steady (if available)
- Two pieces of Styrofoam for the animation

Explain to students that today the class is making their own movie through a technique called *stop-motion animation*. Tell students that they are going to see firsthand how movies are made and will have the opportunity to tell a story in the process. If you have a projector available, you can show students some stop-motion animation movies or songs, such as *Five little ducks*. This way they will know what they are going to make. If a projector is not available, print out three copies of pictures of the story and place them side by side so that students see the movement in progress.

Give students the two Styrofoam pieces and paint and ask them to decorate the background of their movie.

- **Using a smartphone or another electronic device:** When students have finished, set up your device on a tripod across the background scenery. Ask students to help you choose the main characters – family members that will be the protagonists of this movie. Ask students to think of chores they can ask the family members to do and elicit some ideas. Start the app on your device and make your stop animation movie. If available, you can publish your movie on the school website.
- **Having students act out:** Ask students to stand behind a desk and below the Styrofoam sceneries. Have them hold characters and raise their hands to make them move while their classmates watch. Remind them that their arm and hand is the only thing showing in the scene from their body.

Note to teachers
A great way to demonstrate to the students the basic principles behind stop-motion animation is by bringing to class some classic flipbooks, which use a series of drawings to create an animated cartoon.

DIFFERENTIATED INSTRUCTION

BELOW LEVEL
Technology, arts, and math – Draw arrows to order the story.

Materials and preparation
- Pencils
- Project Book page 21

Ask students to open their Project Book to page 21. Have students name the family members they can see in the story. Then draw their attention to the first scene and ask, *What is happening here?* If students use L1, rephrase their ideas in English. Help them identify what comes next in the story and have them draw an arrow from the first to the second scene. Repeat with the other scenes. Then have students tell the story as a class.
Explain to students that this story represents a short movie, but it is a kind a movie where people don't talk and there is no sound. Tell them that this kind of movie was common many years ago and they were called silent movies.

ABOVE LEVEL
Have students do the procedures explained in *Below level*, but after they talk about what is happening in the first scene, have them work in pairs to draw arrows from the first to the second scene and to the other scenes. Then put two pairs of students together, forming a small group, and have them tell the story by themselves.

Explain to students that this story represents a short movie, but it is a kind a movie where people don't talk and there is no sound. Tell them that this kind of movie was common many years ago and they were called silent movies.

CLOSING

Be a silent-movie actor. Say goodbye.

Divide students into pairs and ask them to think of a chore. Tell them they will be actors in a silent movie, so they can't speak. Have them perform to the class. When the movie is over, their classmates can say what the movie was about, *sweeping the floor*, *putting away toys*.
Then have students say goodbye to you as if they were still acting in a silent movie. They can wave to you and their classmates.

Note to teachers
If available, you can choose a short piece of a silent movie to show to students. You can also have them compare how different they are from today's movies.

Unit 3   25

OPENING

Circle time

Materials and preparation
- A bell
- Puppet
- Visual schedule pictures

Say *hello* to students and invite them to sit in a circle. Encourage them to say *hello* to you and the puppet. Make it answer, *Hello, my friends.*
Then place the visual schedule pictures face down in the circle. Call on a student to turn over a picture and show it to the rest of the class. Elicit the name of the subject. Make the bell chime and ask, *Can you hear the chime?* Elicit, *It's (engineering) time!* Repeat with the other subjects.

Science and arts – Where to?

Materials and preparation
- Audio library – songs

Ask students to say some places they go to with their family. Have them line up sitting on the floor. Play a song they like. Pretend to be the driver of a car they are riding in and ask, *Where to?* Have students say the destinations they would like to go to with their family, *To the park. To the club. To the movies.* Have students sing the song as if they were on a family trip. Pretend to be making a sharp turn and have students move to one side as you make a turn. Say, *Watch out! The park is here!* And pretend you are stopping very quickly, having them copy you.

Learning goals
- Be introduced to the idea that a sharp turn to the right makes students' body fall to the left
- Follow the steps of an engineering design process: ask, imagine, create, improve, reflect
- Fix things to reuse
- Match pictures of people doing chores with their outlines

STEAM subjects
- Science
- Engineering
- Arts
- Math

Thinking skills
Remembering, understanding, applying, analyzing, creating

Main language content
Where are we going? Can you fix it?
Family: *brother, dad, mom, sister*
Chores: *sweep the floor, take out the garbage, wash the dishes*
Numbers: *1-10*

STEAM

ACTIVE LEARNING

Engineering – Thinking of ways to fix items

Materials and preparation
- Band-aids
- Broken brooms (made of a stick and some hay or string)
- Broken toy furniture
- Glue
- Masking tape
- Plastic plates cut in the middle
- Plastic spoons broken in the middle
- Play dough
- Scissors

Show students the broken cutlery, furniture, or anything else that needs fixing or mending that you could collect. Have students look at the materials closely. Ask, *What is it? What do we use it for?* Allow students some time to identify the items and help the class name them. Then ask, *How do you think it broke? Can you fix it? Can we use it again?*

Have students brainstorm ideas on how to fix the items. Take their ideas into consideration. If you see that the students are coming up with a lot of different ideas, start problematizing the ideas so that they can think further.

Divide students into small groups. Give out the broken items and all the fixing tools to students and tell them to consider the following:
1. *How can I fix this item so that I can reuse it?*
2. *How can I avoid breaking this item again?*

Have students think and start fixing. Allow them to use the tape, glue, play dough, or anything else they think is best and that you have available.

> **Note to teachers**
> Besides practicing their engineering skills, in this activity students learn about reusing and fixing things so that they don't need to buy new ones.

Engineering – How can I make this fixing better?

Materials and preparation
- Students' fixed items

Have students show their items and explain the suggestions to fix them. Then ask, *How can we make the fixing better?* Have students brainstorm ideas on ways to improve each of the fixed items. Allow students to be creative and always encourage them to participate with their ideas. Students might propose using a different material to make the fixing more discrete or stronger, for example.

DIFFERENTIATED INSTRUCTION

BELOW LEVEL
Math – Look at the outlines. Stick and say.

Materials and preparation
- Project Book page 23
- Unit 3 Stickers

Have students open their Project Book to page 23. Tell them to look at the outlines. Say the chores and have them guess what chore it is, *taking out the garbage, sweeping the floor, washing the dishes*. Then help students peel off the stickers, one by one, and help them identify which outline they belong to. When they finish, help them name the chores.

ABOVE LEVEL

Have students open their Project Book to page 23. Tell them to look at the outlines and say what they think the people are doing: *taking out the garbage, sweeping the floor, washing the dishes*. Tell them to look at the stickers and think of which outline they belong to. Have students check their answers with a classmate and name the chores they see.

CLOSING

Throw the paper ball. Take out the garbage. Say goodbye.

Materials and preparation
- Old magazines or newspapers
- Two baskets with a bag inside

Have students make paper balls from old newspapers or magazines. Divide them into two groups and have them try to throw the paper balls into their group's basket from a distance. When all members in a group have thrown their paper balls, help them check how many there are and ask, *Can you help me? Let's take out the garbage!* Invite a student to collect and close the bag.

Say *goodbye* to students and have them say *goodbye* to you.

HELP MOMMY DUCK FIND HER LITTLE DUCKS. COUNT AND SAY.

STEAM • HOW CAN YOU HELP YOUR FAMILY AT HOME? • UNIT 3 25

Learning goals
- Learn about ducks' habitat
- Count backwards from five to one
- Plan, design, and make binoculars
- Develop problem-solving skills and introduce computational thinking
- Reenact a duck family rhyme

STEAM subjects
- Science
- Technology
- Engineering
- Arts
- Math

Thinking skills
Remembering, understanding, applying, analyzing, creating, evaluating

Main language content
How many ducks came back? Where are the ducks? Four little ducks. It's Mommy Duck.
My binoculars are brown. I can see five little ducks.
Numbers: 1-5

OPENING

Circle time

Materials and preparation
- A bell
- A book
- Puppet
- Visual schedule pictures

Say *hello* to students. Encourage them to say *hello* to you and the puppet. Make it answer, *Hello, my friends.*
Cover the pictures of today's schedule using a book. Hold the pictures behind the book and show part of them only. Ask students if they can guess what activity it is. Repeat with the other picture.
Show one picture at a time, make the bell chime, and ask, *Can you hear the chime?*
Elicit, *It's (arts) time!* Repeat with the other subjects.

Arts – The duck scenery

Materials and preparation
- Colored pencils
- *Five little ducks* video (or song)
- Scenery: a pond, hills, and grass made out of white craft paper, five little ducks made out of sturdy cardboard paper

Bring the nursery rhyme scenery and ducks forward and show them to students. Teach the vocabulary using these props. Elicit any vocabulary they may know and make sure they understand the words *ducks, little ducks,* and *Mommy Duck*. Ask them questions such as *How many ducks are there? What color are the ducks? The hills? The pond? Can you help me color them?*
Give out colored pencils and allow students to color the props using pencils. While they are doing this, play or sing *Five little ducks*.
T: *Five little ducks went swimming one day, over the hills and far away. Mommy Duck said?*
S: *Quack, quack, quack!*
T: *But only four ducks came back.*
Continue the nursery rhyme by changing the number of ducks.

ACTIVE LEARNING

Arts and math – Sing and count down the ducks using your fingers.

Materials and preparation
- Audio library – songs
- Mommy Duck and five little ducks scenery from previous activity
- Online animated video and projector (optional)

Sing the nursery rhyme *Five little ducks* (track 16) with the class. You can also play an online animated video for them. Start with all ducks in the pond and as the story goes on, count and move the ducks over the hills subtracting one and moving the rest back. First, leave one duck over the hills and return with four. Continue until no ducks come back. Finally, when there are no more little ducks, Mommy Duck calls and they all come back! All five little ducks with Mommy Duck back in the pond!
As you set the scene to students, have them show the numbers with their fingers, lowering a finger every time a duck doesn't come back.

Technology and math – Help Mommy Duck find her little ducks. Count and say.

Materials and preparation
- Pencils
- Project Book page 25

Have students open their Project Book to page 25. Ask, *Where is Mommy Duck? Are the little ducks with Mommy Duck? Where are they?* Ask students to use their "writing finger" to trace the path from Mommy Duck to her little ducks. Allow them to try the three paths; then elicit which path helps Mommy Duck get to her little ducks. Then have them make the same path using a pencil.
Ask, *Is the path correct? Is Mommy Duck with her ducks now?* If students haven't gotten to the little ducks, remind them to keep trying and testing their hypotheses.

> **Note to teachers**
> Mazes are problem-solving and pre-computational thinking activities as a specific path must be followed in order to accomplish the expected result.

DIFFERENTIATED INSTRUCTION

BELOW LEVEL
Science, engineering, and arts – Make your own binoculars.

Materials and preparation
- Crayons
- Empty toilet tubes (two per student)
- Feathers
- Googly eyes (or eyes cutouts)
- Little ducks from scenery in previous activities
- Markers
- Sequins
- Tape
- String

Ask students, *What are binoculars? What are they for?* Help them with the answer, if needed.
Give two toilet tubes to each student and have them tape the toilet tubes together and decorate them to make their own binoculars. Put the little ducks all around the pond with some hiding behind the bushes. Ask students to help Mommy Duck find her little ducks.
Talk to students about the ducks' habitat. Ask, *Where do ducks live? Can they fly high?* If nobody comes up with an answer, tell students that ducks live mostly near bodies of water, like rivers, streams, and lakes. Have students look at the ducks using their binoculars and describe the ducks, saying their size, color, and any other information they know.

ABOVE LEVEL
Instead of telling students the steps to make the binoculars as it is in *Below level*, show students the materials and tell them that they are going to be used to make binoculars. Have them work in pairs trying to figure out a way of setting the materials together and making the binoculars. Help as needed. Once they are ready, have students use the binoculars to look at the ducks and say as many things as they can about them.

CLOSING

Act out the nursery rhyme. Say goodbye.

First have students count backwards from five to one. Then sing the nursery rhyme *Five little ducks* very slowly with their help and have students act out the song in groups of six. If necessary, have students join more than one group when acting out. Then say *goodbye* to students and have them say *goodbye* to you, too.

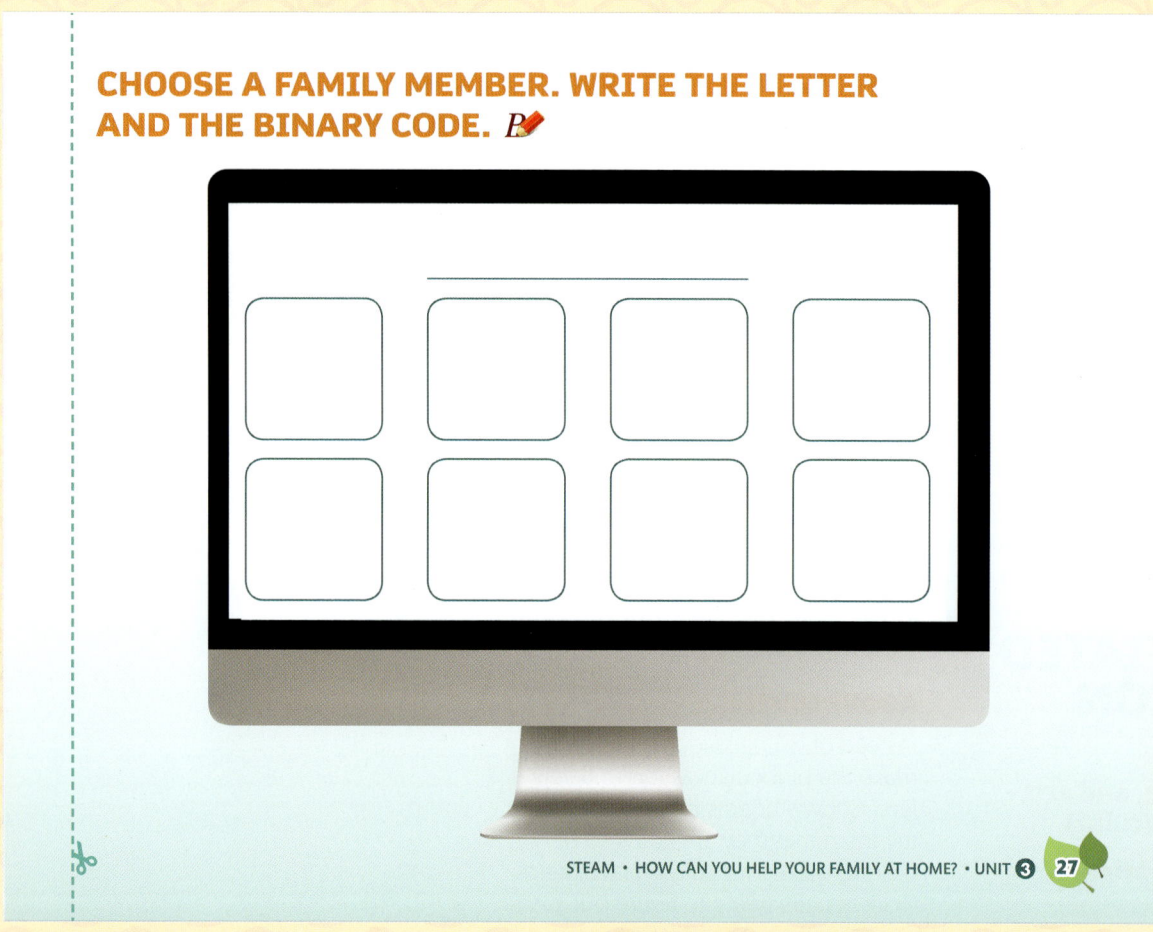

Learning goals
- Encode letters into the binary code
- Make a binary bracelet
- Order people in a family from the shortest to the tallest
- Learn that binary codes are made from ones and zeros, and write a letter using binary code
- Relate binary code to computer language

STEAM subjects
- Technology
- Arts
- Math

Thinking skills
Remembering, understanding, applying, analyzing, creating, evaluating

Main language content
It's a computer. Zero-one-zero-zero.
A bracelet for my grandpa!
It's M for mom. It's D for dad.
Family: *brother, dad, grandma, grandpa, mom, sister*
Colors: *black, blue, brown, green, orange, pink, purple, red, yellow*

OPENING

Circle time

Materials and preparation
- A bell
- Puppet
- Visual schedule pictures

Say *hello* to students. Encourage them to say *hello* to you and the puppet. Make it answer, *Hello, my friends.*
Hide the pictures representing today's schedule and have students look for them. Then have students sit in a circle and place the pictures in the circle. Make the bell chime and say, *Can you hear the chime?*
Show a picture of one of today's activities and elicit, *It's (technology) time!* Repeat with the other subjects.

Technology and math – Hear it and tap it.

Write numbers 0 and 1 on the board within students' reach. Have them make a line. Point to number 0 and elicit the word for the number. Point to 1 and elicit the word for the word. Explain to students the amount represented by zero using your hand. Compare with one and show your index finger. Then tell students they are going to play a game.
Call out a number for each student in a random order and have the first student in line run to the number and tap it. Keep it fast-paced and fun.

> **Note to teachers**
> Teaching the basics of the binary code to young learners helps them learn how to work with computer programs. The binary code is a way of representing information using only two options, 0-1, like *off-on*.

STEAM

ACTIVE LEARNING

Technology and arts – Make a binary decoder key.

Materials and preparation
- Colored markers
- Glue
- Poster paper divided into 26 squares (or two pieces of poster with 13 squares in each)
- Sheets of paper

Assign a color and a letter to each student. If you have a small group, assign two letters and colors to a few students. Have them take that color marker and give them a sheet of paper. Explain that they are going to make a poster that will help them make a gift for someone in their family later. Have students write the letter they were assigned. Help those who find this task difficult.

Ask all students to write the numbers in the sequence you tell them. Tell everyone to start with a *zero*, then a *one*, then two *zeros*. After that tell each student how their numbers should continue (check Note to teachers). When they finish, explain that these numbers represent the letters they wrote. Say, *This is what we call a binary code, it is the language computers use to write*. When students finish, call out the letters of the alphabet in order and ask students to identify which letter they have. Students who are called should come to the poster and place their code there with glue. Call out a few letters, have students identify which letter it is and its color, and ask them to say the binary representation: *L, zero-one-zero-zero-one-one-zero-zero*. Place the poster on a wall so that all students can see it.

> **Note to teachers**
> The alphabet in binary code:
> A – 01000001   N – 01001110
> B – 01000010   O – 01001111
> C – 01000011   P – 01010000
> D – 01000100   Q – 01010001
> E – 01000101   R – 01010010
> F – 01000110   S – 01010011
> G – 01000111   T – 01010100
> H – 01001000   U – 01010101
> I – 01001001   V – 01010110
> J – 01001010   W – 01010111
> K – 01001011   X – 01011000
> L – 01001100   Y – 01011001
> M – 01001101   Z – 01011010

Technology – Choose a family member. Write the letter and the binary code.

Materials and preparation
- Colored pencils
- Project Book page 27

Ask students to think of a family member they would like to give a gift to. Elicit the name of different family members. When they have said the word for a family member, say, for example, *Dad starts with...?* Have students say *D* or make the letter sound. Ask, *What's the code for D?* Repeat with other family members they have chosen.

Have them open their Project Book to page 27 and write the code that represents their letter in the boxes. Then have students exchange codes to check each other's work and write the letter on the line.

DIFFERENTIATED INSTRUCTION

BELOW LEVEL

Technology and arts – Make binary family bracelets.

Materials and preparation
- Beads (two different colors) (about six beads per student),
- Building blocks
- Pipe cleaners or thread

Show students the beads and decide which color is for *one* and which color is for *zero*.
Tell students today you will be making a gift to take home to their families. For this reason, it is important for them to choose a family member they will like to give the bracelet to. Have students say the words for family members and choose the same they chose for the previous activity or a new one.
Then have them look at the poster and choose the beads to make the letter. Have them order the beads first. Then give them the thread and have them place the beads one by one in the order they were before.
Help them make knots on either side of the code and invite students to show their bracelets to their classmates, *A bracelet for my sister!*

> **Note to teachers**
> You can replace the beads with buttons. Make sure to set rules when working with beads or other small materials.

ABOVE LEVEL

Have students do the same as explained in *Below level*, but have them try to figure out the first letter of the family member word they chose by themselves and order the beads alone, too. Monitor their work and see if the help proposed in *Below level* is needed for any students. Invite them to show their work to their classmates, *It's a bracelet for my brother!*

CLOSING

Math – Order the family. Say goodbye.

Materials and preparation
- Magazine cutouts of people

Have students work in groups. Tell them to choose two people from the cutouts to form a family. Have them talk to their classmates about who they think that person is in the family and order the people cutouts in their group from the shortest to the tallest. Monitor their work and help as needed. Allow fast-finishers to check their classmates' work and help. Have students say *goodbye* to the families they created and to you.

Unit 3 | 31

Unit 4 Why do you feel hot or cold?

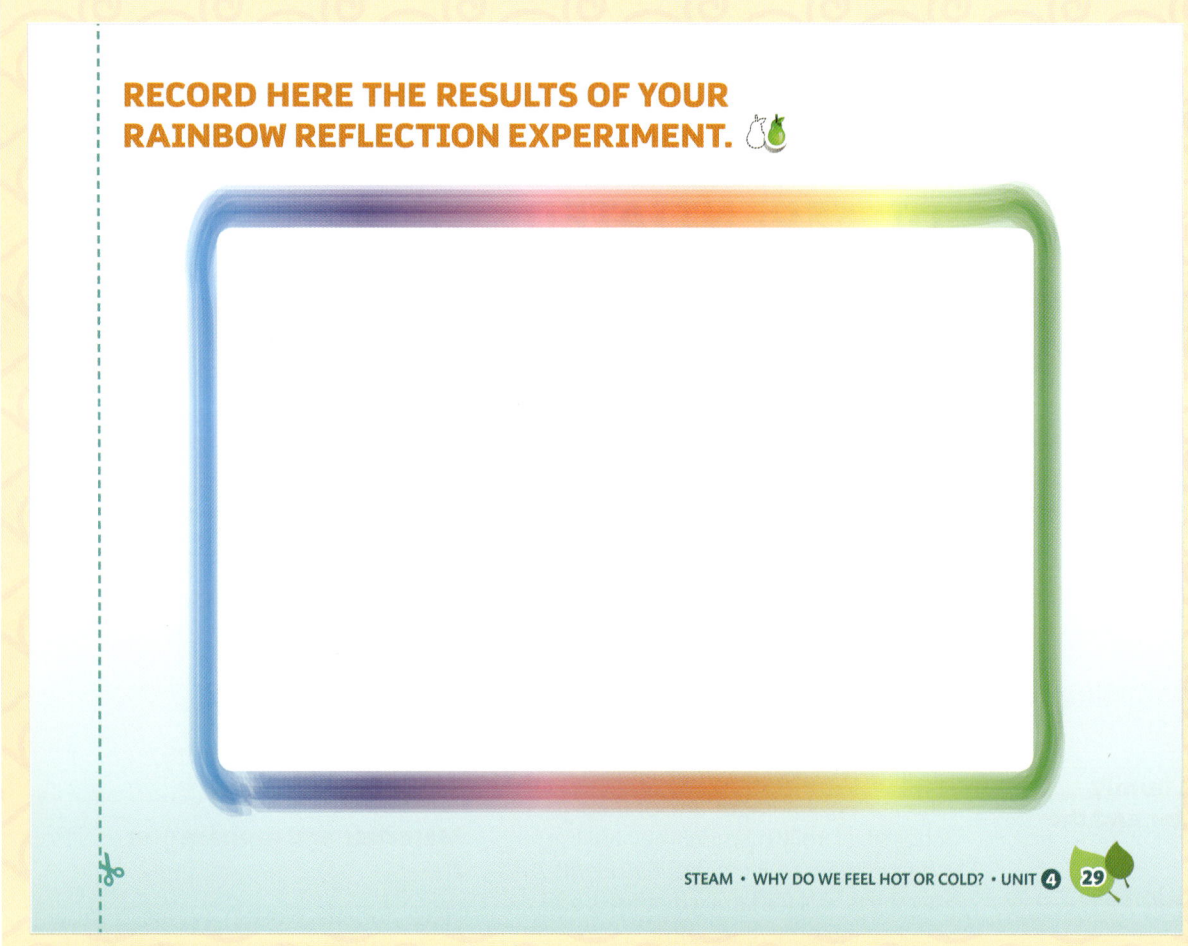

RECORD HERE THE RESULTS OF YOUR RAINBOW REFLECTION EXPERIMENT.

STEAM • WHY DO WE FEEL HOT OR COLD? • UNIT 4 29

Learning goals
- Talk about the colors of the rainbow and make rainbow slime
- Improve concentration and the ability to find similarities in colors through a memory game
- Understand the concept of light reflection through an experiment
- Identify two of the main elements of art: color and texture
- Use a technological device to record the results of an experiment (if available)

STEAM subjects
- Science
- Technology
- Arts
- Math

Thinking skills
Conceptualizing, applying, analyzing, creating, evaluating, improving

Main language content
It's a rainbow. It has seven colors.
What are the colors?
Colors: *blue, green, indigo, orange, red, violet, yellow*

OPENING

Circle time

Materials and preparation
- A bell
- Visual schedule pictures

Have all the students sit in a circle, facing you. Greet them and invite them to greet you back. Review the procedures for gathering in a circle.
Hide the pictures representing today's schedule and have students look for them. Then place them in the circle. Use the attention-getter to introduce today's schedule. Make the bell chime and ask, *Can you hear the chime?* Ask students if they remember how to reply and help as needed.
Show a picture of one of today's activities and elicit, *It's (arts) time!* Repeat with the other subjects.

Math – Play the *Rainbow memory game.*

Materials and preparation
- Crayons or colored pencils (blue, green, indigo, orange, red, violet, yellow)
- Small pieces of craft paper cut into squares (one per student)

Divide students into two groups. Give each student a card and assign them a color. Teach any colors they may not know. Make sure to assign the same colors in both groups so that you have a pair of each color. Tell students to draw a circle and color it using the color they were assigned.
Ask students to sit in a circle. Have them all play a memory game together by placing the two sets of cards facing down in the middle of the circle and picking cards to match. Once they match the cards, they need to call out the color in order to keep the cards.

> **Note to teachers**
> Besides increasing short-term memory and concentration, memory games provide students with the opportunity to improve the ability to find similarities in objects.

32 STEAM

ACTIVE LEARNING

Science and arts – Make rainbow slime.

Materials and preparation
- Baking soda
- Contact lens solution or sodium borate (teacher's use only)
- Food coloring in the rainbow colors (or mix primary colors)
- One bottle of clear glue (150 ml)
- Plastic spoons
- Six small cups

Ask students, *What is a rainbow? How do rainbows form?* Explain that rainbows are formed by sunlight and water particles in the air, so sometimes when it rains and then the sun shines right after, it is possible to see a rainbow.

Tell the class that today you are going to make rainbow slime. Ask if they know what it is and have them share their experience with slime.

Ask for students' help to divide the glue equally into the small cups. Have a student add a pinch of baking soda to each cup and mix it well using a plastic spoon. Have another student drop some food coloring into each cup (a different color for each cup or mixed colors). Lastly, add a large squirt of contact lens solution or half a teaspoon of sodium borate to each cup and mix.

Now invite students to check the slime. Gesture and ask, *Is it too sticky?* Add some more contact lens solution until it feels right but not sticky. Have students use their fingers to massage the slime and mix it better.

When the slime is ready, invite students to make a rainbow! Have students display their rainbows and talk about the colors and the texture of the slime.

> **Note to teachers**
> Take care not to let students put any of these ingredients into their mouth.
> There are many different recipes for slime on the Internet. If time is available, you can try different ingredients for the slime.

Science and technology – Create rainbow reflections.

Materials and preparation
- Blank sheets of paper
- CDs
- Flashlight or sunlight

Divide students into pairs and give each of them a CD. If you have few CDs available, have them share. Ask students if they know what CDs are. Allow them to explore the CD: let them touch it, talk about its shape, what it feels and looks like, etc.

If it is a sunny day, take students outside with the CDs. If not, use a flashlight. Create a reflection by pointing the flashlight onto the CD and having it reflect onto the sheet of paper. Ask students what colors they can see in it. Tell them that this reflection is like a rainbow.

Ask, *How do you think the colors appear on the paper?* Explain that the light is made up of seven colors – like a rainbow – and the material of the CD separates these colors, that's why they see them separately in the reflection.

DIFFERENTIATED INSTRUCTION

BELOW LEVEL
Science and technology – Record here the results of your rainbow reflection experiment.

Materials and preparation
- Camera (optional)
- Glue
- Printer
- Project Book page 29
- Sheets of paper

Have students do the experiment and take a picture of them while holding the flashlight against the CD creating a reflection on the paper.

Ask students to open their Project Book to page 29. You may either have students draw the results of the experiment or print out the pictures they took and have students glue their own picture in the frame. Then have them show their picture to all the class and say the colors they can see in it.

ABOVE LEVEL

Have students do the experiment in pairs and allow them to take a picture of their classmate while doing the experiment. Ask students to open their Project Book to page 29. You may either have students draw the results of the experiment or print out the pictures they took and have students glue their own picture in the frame. Then have them show their picture to a classmate and compare if the colors in their picture are the same as in their classmate's.

> **Note to teachers**
> If a photo camera isn't available, you can have students pose for each other while they draw the results of the experiment in the frame: they can draw the CD, the flashlight, and the paper and color it according to the colors they see.

CLOSING

Play *Tug of peace*. Say goodbye.

Materials and preparation
- Camera (optional)
- Hula hoops (if possible, with different colors)

Take students outside or make space in the classroom. Then divide them into groups. Have groups sit down in circles and put a hula hoop in the middle of each of them. Students need to grab hold of the hoop with both hands and try to stand up together. Help students and be part of a group first to model the activity.

When they finish, you can register their teamwork in pictures on in a video. Ask, *Can the (blue) team stand up? Congratulations! No? Let's help them.*

Then take students back to the classroom and have them say *goodbye* to each other and to you.

Unit 4

WHICH THERMOMETER SHOWS COLD WEATHER? CIRCLE.

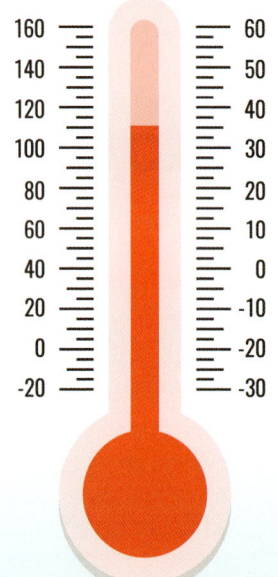 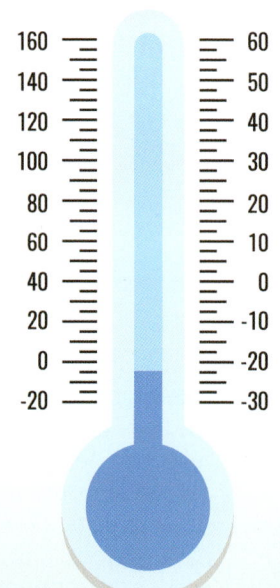

STEAM • WHY DO WE FEEL HOT OR COLD? • UNIT 4

Learning goals
- Identify different types of weather
- Identify different thermometers
- Make a thermometer for their classroom
- Learn how to identify the rise in temperature in a thermometer

STEAM subjects
- Science
- Technology
- Engineering

Thinking skills
Understanding, applying, analyzing, creating, evaluating, improving

Main language content
It's a thermometer. It measures the temperature. The liquid goes up. The liquid goes down. It's rainy. It's hot. It's cold.
Weather: *cold, hot, rainy, snowy, sunny*

 STEAM

OPENING

Circle time

Materials and preparation
- A bell
- Puppet
- Visual schedule pictures
- Weather chart

Say *hello* to students and invite them to sit in a circle. Encourage them to say *hello* to you and the puppet. Make it answer, *Hello, my friends*.
Then place the visual schedule pictures face down in the circle. Use the Weather chart to talk to students about the weather. Ask, *What's the weather like today?* and have them identify the weather by looking through the window.
Call on a student to turn over a picture and show it to the rest of the class. Elicit the name of the subject. Make the bell chime and ask, *Can you hear the chime?* Elicit, *It's (engineering) time!* Repeat with the other subjects.

Science – Play *Roll it.*

Materials and preparation
- Large die
- Pictures of different kinds of weather on each side of the die
- Masking tape

Before class, use masking tape to place the weather cards on each side of the die.
Show students all sides of the die and elicit the weather in each picture. Tell them that they will have to roll the die and, depending on the picture, name the weather condition the weather and say what they would be wearing. For example, *It's cold. I'm wearing a jacket.*

ACTIVE LEARNING

Technology – Learn about thermometers.

Materials and preparation

- Different kinds of real thermometers (or their pictures)
- Pictures of different devices to measure the temperature (optional – you can project them or print them out)

Show students different kinds of real thermometers as an introduction to this activity. Ask, *What are these used for?* Help them understand that they all measure temperature. Explain that there are digital ones, ones that go under their armpits, others that take your temperature just by aiming it at the forehead, others that go into the ear, and other kinds, too.
Ask, *What kind of thermometer do you use at home? What for?* They might refer to those to measure ambient temperature, those for food temperature (in the fridge), and those to measure body temperature. You can use pictures to help students identify the thermometers and think if they have any at home.

Technology and engineering – Make a homemade thermometer.

Materials and preparation

- A clear straw
- Food coloring
- Glass bottle
- Play dough
- Marker
- Rubbing alcohol
- Water

Tell students that today they are making their own thermometer.
Have students help you in the making. First, ask someone to help you fill a quarter (1/4) of the bottle with water and then add an equal amount of rubbing alcohol.
Then hold the bottle and have a student drop in a bit of food coloring. Ask for another student to put the straw into the bottle but hold it suspended in the liquid so that it does not touch the bottom. Ask them to help you wrap the play dough around the top of the bottle and the straw (thus keeping it suspended in place).
Invite students to observe how far up the straw the liquid now comes. Use a marker to mark on the outside of the bottle the spot where the liquid stops filling the straw. This line shows the temperature where you are.
Take the bottle outside and encourage students to observe whether the liquid goes up or down. Challenge students to guess why this happens.
Explain to students that in warm temperatures the liquid will go up and in cold temperatures it will go down.

Note to teachers
The science behind the homemade thermometer: the liquid in the bottle expands (gets bigger) when it is warm and contracts (gets smaller) when it is cold.

DIFFERENTIATED INSTRUCTION

BELOW LEVEL
Science – Which thermometer shows cold weather? Circle.

Materials and preparation

- Pencils
- Project Book page 31

Have students open their Project Book to page 31. Ask, *How many thermometers? How are they different? Which one shows cold weather?* Have students circle the thermometer showing cold weather.

ABOVE LEVEL

Have students answer the questions and do the same as explained in *Below level*, but after that, ask students to talk to a classmate and find two things in the picture that show the differences between the thermometers. They should be able to notice that the cold thermometer is blue and has the colored bar lower.

Note to teachers
Students might ask about the numbers on both sides of the thermometers. Explain that those numbers show temperature, but they are different ways of measuring it. Say that the higher the number the hotter the weather.

CLOSING

Play *What's the weather like?* Say goodbye.

Tell students they are going to play a mime game. Have them ask, *What's the weather like?* Say, for example, *It's rainy and cold.*, and have students pretend to be in the rain and feeling cold. Repeat with other weather words.
Then say *goodbye* to students and encourage them to say *goodbye* to you.

Learning goals
- Do an experiment and see how white clothes protect them from heat
- Make hypotheses before checking results

STEAM subjects
- Science
- Math

Thinking skills
Remembering, understanding, applying, analyzing, creating

Main language content
What am I wearing? Which bottle is hot? Which bottle is cold?
Clothes: *coat, dress, pants, shirt, shoes, shorts, skirt, sweater, T-shirt*
Colors: *black, white*
Weather: *cold, hot*

OPENING

Circle time

Materials and preparation
- A bell
- A book
- Puppet
- Visual schedule pictures

Say *hello* to students. Encourage them to say *hello* to you and the puppet. Make it answer, *Hello, my friends.*
Cover the pictures of today's schedule using a book. Hold the pictures behind the book and show part of them only. Ask students if they can guess what activity it is. Repeat with the other picture.
Show one picture at a time, make the bell chime, and ask, *Can you hear the chime?*
Elicit, *It's (arts) time!* Repeat with the other subjects.

Test your memory.

Materials and preparation
- A blanket (optional)

Stand in front of the class and have them describe what you are wearing. After they have finished, cover yourself with a blanket or have them turn their back to you. Invite them to recall and tell you what you are wearing.
Have students do this activity again, but this time in pairs. Have a student say what their classmate is wearing, turn their back to them, and then try to remember what their classmate is wearing. You can also ask them if they remember the color of the clothes.

ACTIVE LEARNING

Science – White clothes and heat

Materials and preparation
- One liter of black coffee at room temperature
- Sunlight or flashlight
- Tape
- Food thermometer
- Two empty plastic bottles with caps
- White paper

Bring out the material necessary for the experiment and explain to students that they are going to help you do an experiment.
Have students fill each of the plastic bottles up three quarters of the way with the black coffee at room temperature and use the thermometer to check if the temperature of the liquid in the bottles is even.
Make a note of the temperature on the board or on a piece of paper, close the bottles well, and use white paper and tape to wrap one of them.
Leave both bottles in the sun for an hour or with a flashlight closely pointing at one of them.

Note to teachers
Make sure not to use a flashlight with LED bulbs as they do not get warm.

Science – Making hypotheses and checking

Ask students to discuss what they think is going to happen with each bottle. Use some questions to elicit the discussion: *What will happen to the coffee in one hour? Will the liquid in both bottles have the same temperature after an hour? If not, which one do you think is going to have cooler coffee? Why would one of the bottles have a different temperature?*
After an hour, check the temperature of the coffee in both bottles and write down the numbers next to your previous notes. *Which coffee is warmer? Which one is cooler? Why?*
Explain to the class that the coffee bottle wrapped up with the white paper is cooler because the color white reflects heat, while darker colors, such as black, tend to absorb heat. This is the reason why they should wear light-colored clothes during the summer months, to stay cooler.

Note to teachers
In order to leave the bottles enough time in the sun, you can do the following activities first and then come back to this one.

DIFFERENTIATED INSTRUCTION

BELOW LEVEL
Math – Cut out the pictures. Play a sorting-out game.

Materials and preparation
- Project Book page 33
- Scissors

Have students open their Project Book to page 33 and cut out the pictures. Have them work in pairs to sort the clothes according to the temperature they are worn – *hot* or *cold*. Then have pairs play a memory game together.

ABOVE LEVEL
Have students do the same procedures described in *Below level*, but have them sort out the pictures individually and name the pieces of clothing before playing the memory game.

Note to teachers
Children at this age are still learning to cut with scissors, so this activity is a great opportunity to encourage them to practice it, as they are required to cut along lines only. Nevertheless, make sure to help students as needed.

CLOSING

Play *Walk, walk, walk... Stop!* Say goodbye.

Materials and preparation
- Black cards and white cards (one of either per student, an even number of the same color)
- Puppet

Give a card to each student. Have them walk as you chant, *Walk, walk, walk, walk...* Then say *stop* and have students stand in front of another classmate and say what color they have. If they have the same color, they can sit down together and watch the others play. Go on until everyone has found a peer.
Then have students say *goodbye* to their classmates, to you, and the puppet.

MAKE A NATURE ARTWORK.

STEAM • WHY DO WE FEEL HOT OR COLD? • UNIT 4 • 35

Learning goals
- Talk about the colors of leaves
- Investigate why leaves change color
- Make an artwork by rubbing a crayon on a leaf
- Group items by color

STEAM subjects
- Science
- Arts
- Math

Thinking skills
Remembering, understanding, applying, analyzing

Main language content
Why does it happen? What's the weather like today?
It's raining. It's sunny.
Four orange leaves.
Colors: *brown, green, orange, yellow*
Numbers: *1-10*

OPENING

Circle time

Materials and preparation
- A bell
- Puppet
- Visual schedule pictures

Say *hello* to students. Encourage them to say *hello* to you and the puppet. Make it answer, *Hello, my friends.*
Hide the pictures representing today's schedule and have students look for them. Then have students sit in a circle and place the pictures in the circle. Make the bell chime and say, *Can you hear the chime?*
Show a picture of one of today's activities and elicit, *It's (science) time!* Repeat with the other subjects.

Science and arts - What's the weather like today?

Materials and preparation
- Contact paper or a piece of transparent plastic as large as the classroom glass window
- Cotton
- Raindrops and sun cutouts
- Tape

Place the contact paper on a class window with the sticky part facing you or use tape to stretch the transparent plastic. Give students cotton and the sun and raindrop cutouts and have them make the weather of the day. Ask them to say where they want each of the things to go and help them place the pictures if the window is high. Then ask, *What's the weather like?*

STEAM

ACTIVE LEARNING

Science – Learning about leaves

Materials and preparation
- Several leaves from outside of different colors

Talk to students about the leaves you have brought into class. Elicit the colors of the leaves and their similarity to shapes they know (oval, hexagon, etc.).
Explain to students that you picked up these leaves from the ground.
Ask, *Why do leaves fall? Why do they change color?*
Allow some time for students to think and expose their ideas. All opinions are accepted; after all, they are brainstorming possibilities.

> **Note to teachers**
> Try to find the leaves on the ground. If you need to take them from living plants, then take just a few.

Science – Why do leaves change color?

Materials and preparation
- A jar
- A small bowl
- A disposable coffee filter
- Plastic wrap
- Rubbing alcohol
- Scissors (teacher use only)
- Three green leaves (from the same tree)

Tell students that today they are going to do an experiment to see why leaves change color.
1. Ask for students' help to break the leaves into small pieces and put them in the jar.
2. Pour the alcohol over the leaves until they are just covered.
3. Have students mash and mix the leaves with their hands until the liquid turns greenish.
4. Cover the jar with the plastic wrap and place it in a bowl with hot water in it.
5. Leave for thirty minutes, shaking the jar a little to stir the leaves.
6. When the liquid turns very dark green, cut a strip from the coffee filter and place it inside the jar vertically, like a straw.
7. Have students observe how the liquid travels up the coffee filter and evaporates leaving just the colors on it.
Ask, *What colors do you see on the coffee strip? Aren't they the colors leaves turn to?* Students might see the colors yellow, brown, red, and orange.
Explain to students that it is something called chlorophyll that gives leaves their green color. It is such a dominant substance that it hides the other colors in the leaves. When the weather gets colder, it breaks down and allows the other colors to appear.

DIFFERENTIATED INSTRUCTION

BELOW LEVEL
Science, arts, and math – Make a nature masterpiece.

Materials and preparation
- Crayons
- Leaves (several sizes and colors, one per student or have them share)
- Project Book page 35

Have students open their Project Book to page 35. Tell them to look at the frame on the page and say what they see: *leaves*. Explain that they will make a nature artwork with crayons and leaves. Give students a leaf and have them place the page over it, so that the frame is exactly over the leaf. Tell them to choose a color of crayon and rub its long side on the area over the leaf. Ask, *What can you see in the colored parts?* They will notice that the colored areas are forming a leaf.
Divide students into small groups and have them compare the colors they chose for their leaf and count how many of each there are in their groups.

ABOVE LEVEL
Have students do the same activity described in *Below level*, but when their artwork is finished, divide them into two groups and have them group their work first according to color, then according to size and shape.

CLOSING

Do a gallery walk. Say goodbye.

Materials and preparation
- Students' artworks
- Tape

Use tape to display students' artworks on the wall. Have students do a gallery walk. Remind them of the procedures for walking safely and not crowding their classmates.
As they walk and look at their work, allow them to talk about the colors they see, the size of the leaf, and say which one they like best.
Say *goodbye* to students and have them wave and say *goodbye* to you, too.

Unit 5 What other living things are around us?

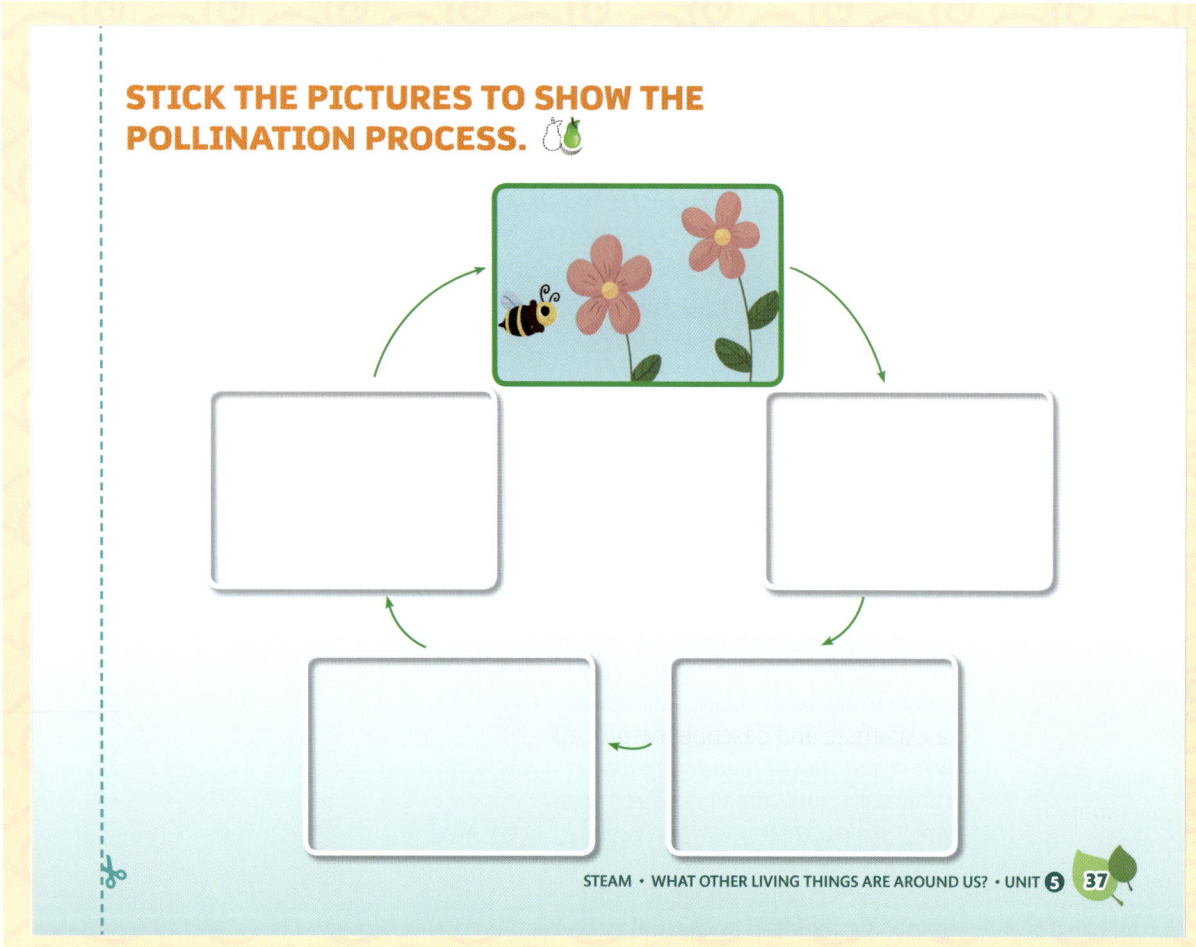

OPENING

Circle time

Materials and preparation
- A bell
- Visual schedule pictures

Have all the students sit in a circle, facing you. Greet them and invite them to greet you back. Review the procedures for gathering in a circle.
Hide the pictures representing today's schedule and have students look for them. Then place them in the circle.
Call on a student to be the class helper and give the bell to them. Have them make the bell chime and ask, *Can you hear the chime?* Ask students if they remember how to reply and help as needed.
Show a picture of one of today's activities and elicit, *It's (arts) time!* Repeat with the other subjects.

Arts – Dancing bees

Materials and preparation
- Chalk or masking tape

Take students outside or make space in the classroom. Use chalk or masking tape to make several X marks on the floor. Tell the class that you are going to pretend to be bees dancing and you need to pass through the marks on the floor. Have students line up and start skipping from one mark to the other. You can have the others count as their classmate is going through the path.

Learning goals
- Talk about pollination and make an experiment to see how it works
- Work on a sequence to help a bee pollinate flowers
- Understand that when the process is not correctly ordered, it might affect the result

STEAM subjects
- Science
- Technology
- Math

Thinking skills
Conceptualizing, understanding, applying, analyzing, creating

Main language content
The bee collects the pollen. It flies to the next flower.
Plants: *bee, flower, plant, pollination, oxygen*

ACTIVE LEARNING

Science – Learning about pollination

Materials and preparation
- A plant or a picture of a plant

Show students a plant and elicit what it is. Ask students what they know about plants. Have them talk about the different sizes and colors they can find. Ask, *Do you know how plants grow? Why do bees land on plants? What do they take and what do they give the plant?*
Explain to students that flowers produce a substance called pollen and that bees transfer this pollen from one flower to the other with their dance. Say, *This is called pollination.* Ask, *What happens when a flower gets pollinated?* Explain to students that it produces seeds and fruit.

Science – Make a pollination representation.

Materials and preparation
- Cotton balls (three per group)
- Cotton swabs (one per group)
- Cupcake liners (three per group)
- Cups with water
- Three colors of glitter

Divide students into groups and give each group a set of the materials requested. Put the cupcake liners one next to the other and place a cotton ball in each. Sprinkle some glitter of different colors on each cotton ball. Have students wet the cotton swab and squeeze it to get the excess water off it. Have a student from each group gently rub the cotton swab onto the first cotton ball, picking up some glitter, and then onto the other two cotton balls. Ask students what they have observed and what each part represents (glitter is pollen, each cupcake liner is a flower, and the cotton swab is the bee). Ask students again, *Why do plants and animals need each other?*

Note to teachers
Children at this age usually need a visualization of the concept they are being taught in order to fully grasp it, so make sure to tell them what each of the materials represent in the pollination process.

DIFFERENTIATED INSTRUCTION

BELOW LEVEL
Science, technology, and math – Stick the pictures to show the pollination process.

Materials and preparation
- Project Book page 37
- Unit 5 Stickers

Have students open their Project Book to page 37.
Help students identify the order of the events according to the direction of the arrows. Show them the first picture. Say, *This bee is pollinating the flowers. Let's see how it does this?* Have them look the Unit 5 stickers at the end of their Project Book and describe each of the pollination steps for them to identify the correct sticker, peel it off, and place it in the box. Then have everyone describe each of the stages in the process of pollination according to the pictures.

Note to teachers
In this activity students will be using their knowledge of sequencing to help the bee pollinate the flowers. Remind students that, if they misplace the stickers, the process will be incorrect and, therefore, pollination won't happen.

ABOVE LEVEL
Have students do the same activity described in *Below level*, but instead of saying each of the stages in the pollination process, allow them to figure them out by themselves and stick the pictures in the correct place. When they finish, have them work with a classmate and describe the process. Then check as a class, having all students participate in the telling of the pollination process.

CLOSING

Transfer the pollen. Say goodbye.

Materials and preparation
- Plastic cups, two of them filled with water (one cup per student)

Tell students they are going to pretend to be bees transferring the pollen from one flower to another. Have them form two circles. Give one student in each circle a cup filled with water. Have this student transfer almost all of their water to their classmate's cup, keeping just a little of it in their cup. Have this go on until everyone in the group has a little water in each of their cups.
Say, *The water is the pollen. The bee carries with it a little bit of pollen it takes from one flower to another flower, and this goes on until all flowers have some pollen from the bees or other insects.*
Have students clean-up and put the cups away. Say *goodbye* to them and have them say *goodbye* to you.

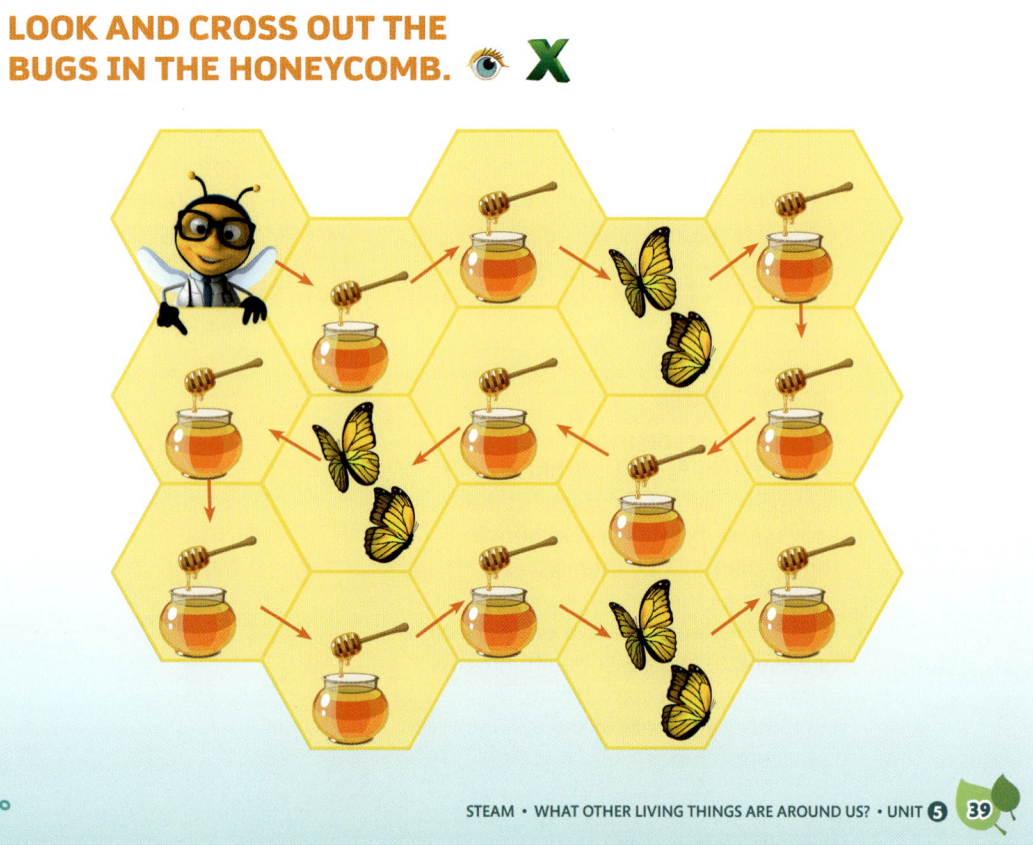

OPENING

Circle time
Materials and preparation
- A bell
- Puppet
- Visual schedule pictures

Say *hello* to students and invite them to sit in a circle. Encourage them to say *hello* to you and the puppet. Make it answer, *Hello, my friends*.
Then place the visual schedule pictures face down in the circle. Call on a student to turn over a picture and show it to the rest of the class. Elicit the name of the subject. Invite a student to make the bell chime and ask, *Can you hear the chime?* Elicit from the rest of the class, *It's (engineering) time!* Repeat with the other subjects.

Science and arts – Make a pollination sensory bin.
Materials and preparation
- Plastic zip-lock bag
- Transparent hair gel (optional)
- Yellow sand

Put the sand into the zip-lock bag. If gel is available, put some, too. Tell students that the content of the bag represents something bees take from one flower to another. *What is it?* Elicit, *It's pollen. It's yellow.*
Have students use their fingers to make drawings or shapes on the "pollen". Elicit what they remember from the pollination process while they are playing.

Learning goals
- Learn about bees and make a craft bee
- Learn that honeycombs are made of hexagon shapes
- Count the hexagons in a honeycomb
- Debug a honeycomb program

STEAM subjects
- Science
- Technology
- Engineering
- Arts
- Math

Thinking skills
Remembering, understanding, applying, analyzing, creating, evaluating

Main language content
What do bees eat? Do you like honey?
It's pollen. It's yellow.
Shapes: *circle, hexagon*
Small animals: *bee, bug, butterfly*
Numbers: *1-15*

STEAM

ACTIVE LEARNING

Science – Learning about and tasting honey

Materials and preparation
- Books with pictures of bees
- Honey
- Plastic spoons

Ask students what they know about bees. *Where do bees live? (in beehives) What do they eat? (honey that they make from the nectar they get from flowers). Are bees good for animals and plants? (Yes, they help in making fruit and seeds).* Show some pictures of bees from the books you have brought. Ask, *Do you like honey?* Give students some honey to taste. *Is it good?*

> **Note to teachers**
> Remember to check for any allergies students might have before giving them honey to taste.

Engineering and arts – Make a bee.

Materials and preparation
- Black markers
- Black string
- Brushes
- Egg cartons cut into twelve parts (one part per student)
- Googly eyes (optional)
- Small pieces of baking paper
- Scissors (age-appropriate)
- White construction paper
- Yellow paint

Tell students you are going to make a bee. Provide them with the materials needed and show them how to use them. Explain that the egg carton is going to be the body, one section for each bee. Have them paint their section with yellow paint and let it dry. While the paint is drying, give students scissors to cut out some small wings from the white construction paper. Help those students who find it difficult to use scissors.

Help students wrap black string around their egg carton to make the stripes of the bee. You can make a small snip at the bottom and slip the string through it. Ask students, *What's missing? How can you make this bee look better?* Elicit some ideas, such as glue googly eyes or paper eyes, make a smile on it, use baking paper for the wings, etc.

> **Note to teachers**
> When using craft material that isn't available in your school, make sure to ask students to bring it from home in the previous class.

DIFFERENTIATED INSTRUCTION

BELOW LEVEL
Technology and math – Look and cross out the bugs in the honeycomb.

Materials and preparation
- Pencils
- Project Book page 39

Have students open their Project Book to page 39, look at the honeycomb, and count the hexagons: *There are fifteen hexagons.*
Next tell them that Dr. Bee is checking on the honey production and that there are some bugs – mistakes – in the honey program. Have them point to each hexagon and say what they see: if they don't see honey, they will cross out that picture. Elicit the name of the animals that are the bugs in the honeycomb program: *butterflies.*

ABOVE LEVEL
Have students follow the procedures explained in *Below level*, but instead of having students point to each and every hexagon before identifying the bugs, have them look at the honeycomb as a whole and try to identify the bugs there. Then ask, *What animal represents a bug in the honeycomb program? Why is it incorrect to have butterflies in the honeycomb program?* Elicit that butterflies are not part of a honeycomb.

CLOSING

Tap the honeycomb hexagons. Say goodbye.

Materials and preparation
- Honeycomb made of ten hexagons (use butcher paper or poster paper)
- Masking tape
- pictures of butterflies, honey, and bees taped on the hexagons (pictures will repeat)

Place the honeycomb on the wall within students' reach. Have students line up in front of it. Call out the name of an item, *bee, honey, butterfly,* and have the student tap the correct picture(s). Have all students play. Keep the game fast-paced and fun.
Have students say *goodbye* and wave at you. Wave back to them and say *goodbye,* too.

Unit 5 | 43

Learning goals
- Understand what a footprint is
- Talk about and compare animal footprints
- Make their classmate's footprint and compare it with another classmate's and an animal's

STEAM subjects
- Science
- Arts
- Math

Thinking skills
Conceptualizing, applying, analyzing

Main language content
It's a bird's footprint. It's a dog's footprint.
It's big. It's small.
It has four toes.
Animals: bird, dog, horse
Numbers: 1-5

OPENING

Circle time

Materials and preparation
- A bell
- Puppet
- Visual schedule pictures

Bring out the puppet and start by having it greet the students. After they greet the puppet, have the puppet greet you, too. Then elicit *Hello!* and ask students how they are today. Show them how to respond using their thumbs.

Hide the pictures representing today's schedule and have students look for them. Ask those who found the pictures to say what they will learn today. Help if needed.

Invite a student to make the bell chime and teach them to ask, *Can you hear the chime?* Show a picture of one of today's activities and elicit, *It's (math) time!* Repeat with the other subjects.

Science and math – What is a footprint?

Materials and preparation
- Two sandboxes with the sand quite wet or some play dough

Have students stand up. Invite one student to take off their shoe and sock and step into the sandbox/onto the play dough. As they take away their foot, have the other students look at the footprint left by their classmate. Show surprise and ask, *What's this?* If students use L1, rephrase their ideas in English English. Explain that the mark our foot leaves in the sand or when our foot is dirty, for example, is called a footprint.

Have another student leave their footprint in the other sandbox/piece of play dough and invite students to compare the feet: *Are they the same? How are they different?* Help students compare the similarities by counting toes, for example, and the differences by comparing sizes.

ACTIVE LEARNING

Science and math – Match the animals with their footprints.

Materials and preparation
- Pencils
- Project Book page 41

Have students open their Project Book to page 41 and elicit the names of the animals. Then have them match the animals with their footprints. Finally tell students to compare the differences in size, shape, and number of toes in the animal footprints.

Arts and math – Make your classmate's footprint.

Materials and preparation
- Washable paint
- Pieces of poster paper (one per student)

Divide students into pairs. Give each student a piece of paper and paint and ask them to take off one of their shoes. Have them help their classmate to put some paint on the sole of their foot and place their foot on the paper. Model first. Have students compare their footprint with their classmate's. Monitor and help as needed. Invite a few pairs to share the differences between their footprints with the rest of the class.

> **Note to teachers**
> Make sure to prepare some pieces of cloth and water for students to clean their feet before putting the shoes back on. You can also take them to the school washing facilities to do that.

DIFFERENTIATED INSTRUCTION

BELOW LEVEL
Science and math – Do a gallery walk.

Materials and preparation
- Masking tape
- Project Book page 41
- Student's footprints

Ask for students' help to place their own footprints and the animal footprints on the wall using tape. Invite them to do a gallery walk. Review the procedures for walking safely around the classroom and remind them not to crowd their classmates.
As they walk, point to a student's footprint and an animal's and ask, *Are they similar? How are they different? How many toes here? And here?*

ABOVE LEVEL

Do the procedures explained in *Below level*, but don't ask any questions while students do the gallery walk. After they have seen all the footprints, divide students into pairs and assign each pair two of the footprints, an animal's and a classmate's. Tell them to think of the differences between the two shapes. They might talk about the number of toes, the sizes, and the shapes in them. Then gather students in a circle and invite them to share the differences they noticed.

CLOSING

Talk about animal footprints. Say goodbye.

Have students sit in a circle to talk about animal footprints. Ask, *Are any of the footprints similar? What footprints have round shapes like a circle? Do you think your footprints are bigger than your mom's/dad's/grandma's? How many toes in the bird's footprint? What about your footprint?* Allow students to talk without checking their books. If necessary, show students your book for them to check their answers. Then wave goodbye to students and encourage them to wave and say *goodbye* to you and the puppet.

Learning goals
- Identify that spiders and insects have a different number of legs
- Identify the spider's problem
- Plan and design improvements for the waterspout
- Count and group spiders and insects

STEAM subjects
- Science
- Technology
- Engineering
- Arts
- Math

Thinking skills
Remembering, understanding, applying, analyzing, creating

Main language content
How many legs? Spiders have eight legs. Insects have six legs. Spiders don't have antennae. Insects have antennae. Go forward. Turn left. Turn right.
Numbers: 1-10

OPENING

Circle time
Materials and preparation
- A bell
- A book
- Puppet
- Visual schedule pictures

Say *hello* to students. Encourage them to say *hello* to you and the puppet. Make it answer, *Hello, my friends.*
Cover the pictures of today's schedule using a book. Hold the pictures behind the book and only show part of them. Ask students if they can guess what activity it is. Repeat with the other picture.
Show one picture at a time, invite a student to make the bell chime, and help them to ask, *Can you hear the chime?*
Elicit from the others, *It's (arts) time!* Repeat with the other subjects.

Science – Spiders and insects
Materials and preparation
- Pictures about insects and spiders

Hide the pictures and have students look for them. When they find the pictures, have them place them in the middle of the circle, facing up.
Ask students what they know about spiders. Ask, *Are spiders insects? Are they small animals? How many eyes? How many legs?* Explain that spiders belong to a different species, they are called arachnids.
Then ask, *What is the difference between a spider and an insect?* Point to the legs of the spider in the picture. Then point to the legs of another insect. Elicit, *Spiders have eight legs. Insects have six legs.* Point to the antennae on the insects and then to the spider's head. Say, *Spiders don't have antennae. Insects have antennae. Some people have spiders as pets.*
Now, ask students which fact they found the most interesting.

46 STEAM

ACTIVE LEARNING

Engineering and arts – Solving the spider problem

Materials and preparation
- Building blocks
- Buttons
- Cardboard boxes and tubes (one of each per group)
- Clay
- Glue
- Lyrics of the nursery rhyme *The Itsy-bitsy spider*.
- Plastic cups and plates (one of each per group)
- Play dough
- Scissors
- String

Sing the song *The Itsy-bitsy spider* with students. Ask, *What is the spider's problem?* Make sure they understand that when it rains, the spider slides down the waterspout. Ask, *How can we help the spider solve this problem?* Divide students into groups, allow time for them to brainstorm ideas, and listen to what they have to say. After you have listened to students' ideas, give them the materials to build something that can help the spider stay put when it rains.
Students' ideas may range from magnetic shoes for the spider (just like a superhero) to climbing holds inside the spout (just like a climbing wall). Allow them to work in groups and try to build their ideas. If any students need to use scissors, help them as needed.

When students have finished, have each group present their solution and how they built it.

Note to teachers
When singing nursery rhymes or telling common stories to children, you can either sing the song/tell the story yourself and use images to help or search for an online video. Make sure to check the language and if it is age-appropriate before showing it.

Engineering – How can you make it better?

Materials and preparation
- Students' work from previous activity

Ask students to leave their work on their table. Have groups change places and look at their classmates' solution. Ask, *How can you make it better?* Allow them to brainstorm ideas. Then have them talk to each other about the ideas they have had. Accept all answers and help students come up with a way of applying their idea. If time allows, you can have them test their improvement in their classmates' work.

DIFFERENTIATED INSTRUCTION

BELOW LEVEL
Science and technology – Help the spider get to the web.

Materials and preparation
- Pencils
- Project Book page 43

Have students open their Project Book to page 43. Invite students to look at the pictures and find the shorter way to help the spider get home. Allow them to use their "writing finger" first. Then tell them to draw the line. Use the following commands to guide students: *go forward, turn left, turn right*.

ABOVE LEVEL

Have students do the procedures explained in *Below level*, but don't give them the commands at first. Use the commands for them to check if the path they took was the shorter. Have them compare their path with a classmate's and say who followed the shorter path.

Note to teachers
Understanding simple directions and learning about shortcuts can help students understand programming language more easily when they start using computers.

CLOSING

Math – Counting legs and counting goodbyes.

Ask students to get together in groups so that they have the same number of legs as a spider in their group. Let them count and realize how many they need to form eight legs.
Then have students in a group say *goodbye*, one at a time, and have groups count the goodbyes in their group. Say *goodbye* to all of them.

Unit 5 | 47

Unit 6 Why is food important?

Learning goals
- Group items according to their use
- Learn how different kinds of soap can make them feel
- Experiment on how different brands of soap can clean their hands
- Learn about the importance of washing their hands before eating

STEAM subjects
- Science
- Math

Thinking skills
Remembering, understanding, applying, analyzing, evaluating

Main language content
Wash your hands. Use soap.
It smells good. It smells bad.
I like it. I don't like it.
Adjectives: *clean, dirty*
Colors: *blue, green, pink, white, yellow*

OPENING

Circle time
Materials and preparation
- A bell
- Puppet
- Visual schedule pictures

Bring out the puppet and start by having it greet the students. After they greet the puppet, have the puppet greet you, too. Then elicit *Hello!* and ask students how they are today. Show them how to respond using their thumbs.

Hide the pictures representing today's schedule and have students look for them. Ask those who found the pictures to say what they will learn today. Help if needed.

Make the bell chime and ask, *Can you hear the chime?* Show a picture of one of today's activities and elicit, *It's (science) time!* Repeat with the other subject.

Science - How are soap bars different?
Materials and preparation
- Different brands of soap

Ask students to sit in a circle. Show them a few different brands of soap. Have them pass the soap around and say if they like the smell, if they smell the same, and talk about their color. When they all have seen the brands, ask, *Do you think all these soap bars clean the same way?* Allow them to make guesses. Remind them of the importance of listening to their classmates.

> **Note to teachers**
> Encouraging students to make guesses is a great way to teach them about hypotheses and raise their curiosity to look for answers.

ACTIVE LEARNING

Science – How does soap clean your hands?

Materials and preparation

- A selection of fruits (check for allergies beforehand)
- Clay (just enough to have students get their hands dirty)
- Different brands of soap
- Paper towels (two per student)
- Water (preferably school washing facilities)

Ask students to put both their hands on the clay so as to get them dirty. Show them the selection of fruits and ask, *Can we eat with our hands looking like this? Why not?* Help students understand that they should have clean hands to eat. Take them to the school washing facility (or bring buckets with water to the classroom) and have students choose a soap to wash their hands until you say *stop*. Have them use a paper towel to wipe their hands and leave the towel aside (do not throw it away). Ask them to repeat the procedure: get hands dirty, wash them for a while, wipe them; except this time have students use another brand of soap.

After that, ask students to take their paper towels back to the classroom and see which of them is dirtier. Have them realize that the other piece of paper towel is cleaner and so, the soap used for that washing is more effective at cleaning their hands.

When students have finished washing their hands, bring out the fruits and say, *Now our hands are clean. Let's eat some fruit.*

Science and math – What can clean your hands? Circle them blue.

Materials and preparation

- Blue pencils
- Project Book page 45

Have students open their Project Book to page 45 and say what they can see in each picture. Say, *Which of these things do you use to clean your hands? Circle them blue.* Have students look at each of the pictures and help them as needed. Allow them to compare answers with a classmate before correcting as a class.

Then have students discuss the items they didn't circle. Ask, *What do they have in common?* Help them understand that those things can make their hands dirty very easily.

DIFFERENTIATED INSTRUCTION

BELOW LEVEL
How are they different?

Materials and preparation

- Paper towels students used to clean their hands

Divide students into pairs. Have them show both their paper towels to their classmate and say which is very dirty. Have them also show which brand of soap they used.

ABOVE LEVEL

Divide students into small groups and have them talk about both their paper towels, saying which is very dirty and which brand they used then. After that, ask students to look at all the towels in the group and say which is the cleanest and which is the dirtiest. Help them with language if needed.

CLOSING

Talk about other uses of soap. Say goodbye.

Materials and preparation

- A piece of clothing that has recently been washed and smells like laundry detergent
- A dish that smells like detergent

Invite students to sit in a circle. Ask them what other uses for soap they know of. Ask, *Do we use soap only to wash our hands?* Students might talk about bathing and showering only, so show them the items and have students smell them. Ask, *What smell is that? How did the smell get there?* Help students understand that soap can be used to wash other things, too. Finally, wave goodbye to students and have them say *goodbye* to you.

RECORD THE PROGRESS OF YOUR EXPERIMENT.

BEFORE	AFTER AN HOUR	THE NEXT DAY

STEAM • WHY IS FOOD IMPORTANT? • UNIT 6 47

Learning goals
- Learn about fruit oxidation
- Do an experiment with fruits and record its progress
- Learn about right and left and play a coder game

STEAM subjects
- Science
- Technology

Thinking skills
Remembering, understanding, applying, analyzing, creating, evaluating

Main language content
Do you like (apples)? Are apples brown?
Will they change color? Will they become bigger?
Go forward. Turn left. Turn right
Food: *apple, banana, carrot, French fries, hamburger, orange, potato, spaghetti, tomato*
Colors: *brown, green, red, yellow*

OPENING

Circle time

Materials and preparation
- A bell
- Visual schedule pictures

Have all the students sit in a circle, facing you. Greet them and invite them to greet you back. Review the procedures for gathering in a circle.
Hide the pictures representing today's schedule and have students look for them. Then place them in the circle.
Call on a student to be the class helper and give the bell to them. Have them make the bell chime and ask, *Can you hear the chime?* Ask students if they remember how to reply and help as needed. Show a picture of one of today's activities and elicit, *It's (technology) time!* Repeat with the other subjects.

Raise your hand for *yes*.

Tell students that you are going to ask them questions and they need to raise their hands if the answer is *yes* and do nothing if the answer is *no*. Ask questions about food and about their food preferences, such as, *Do you like apples? Do you like spaghetti? Are apples brown? Have you ever seen a brown apple?*
Call for a volunteer student to ask two similar questions to his classmates. Then call for another volunteer or pick a student.

 STEAM

ACTIVE LEARNING

Science – Learn about fruit oxidation.

Materials and preparation
- A banana
- A potato
- An apple
- Lemon juice
- Plastic knives
- Small containers (five per group of students)
- Tonic water
- Vinegar
- Water

Divide students into three groups and tell them *It's science time!* Assign a fruit or vegetable to each group. Elicit the names of the food items. Ask, *What do you think we are going to do with each item?*
Give each group five small containers. Give the groups their fruit or vegetable cut in pieces and have them put a few of those pieces in each of the five containers. Put a type of liquid – lemon juice, water, tonic water, or vinegar – in each container and leave one container without any liquid.
Ask, *What do you think will happen?* and let students express their opinions freely. Ask a few questions to help them make hypotheses: *Will the items become smaller? Will they become bigger? Will they change color? Will they lose all color?*
Tell students they will leave the items there for a while.

> **Note to teachers**
> Change the order of activities and check and record the progress of the experiment after about an hour. Make some time the next day in class to record the final result of the experiment.

Science – Record the progress of your experiment.

Materials and preparation
- Colored pencils
- Project Book page 47

Have students open their Project Book to page 47 and take a look at the grid. Explain that this is called *an observation sheet* and it is where they are going to write down what will happen to the items of the experiment. Have students draw five units of their fruit or vegetable under BEFORE, AFTER AN HOUR, and THE NEXT DAY and ask them to color the BEFORE section according to what they see now in the containers.

> **Note to teachers**
> Have students observe the containers and record the results an hour and a day later. They should notice the color change in the fruit and understand that when fruits turn brown, it means that they are going through oxidation. The fruits without liquid and in vinegar turn brown more quickly than the one in water.

Technology – Play *Right or left*.

Materials and preparation
- Chalk or masking tape

Take students outside or make space in the classroom. Draw a line on the floor and write the letters L and R on either side of the line: L on the left and R on the right. Teach students which side means *right* and which side means *left* and have them practice first. Have students stand on one side of the line and jump to the left or right side of the line according to your command, *right* or *left*. You can also call on volunteers to say *right* or *left* for their classmates to jump.

DIFFERENTIATED INSTRUCTION

BELOW LEVEL
Technology – Play the *Coder* game.

Materials and preparation
- Chalk or masking tape
- Flashcards: *apple, carrot, French fries, hamburger, orange, spaghetti, tomato*

Draw a 6x6 grid on the floor using chalk or tape and put a START and an END sign on the grid. Write the letters L and R on the left and on the right side of the grid to help students identify *left* and *right*.
Divide students into small groups and have them play the *Coder* game. Put some food flashcards inside the grid. Tell the students that one is going to be the computer and the other ones from the group are going to be the coders (programmers). The coders use the sequence of commands to make the "computer" pick up some fruit and take them to the end line.
The sequence of commands should go: *forward, left, right*. Help them as needed.

ABOVE LEVEL
Have students do the activity described in *Below level*, but have them use full commands to tell their classmates: *go forward, turn left, turn right*.

CLOSING

Science – Record the progress of your experiment.
Say goodbye.

Materials and preparation
- Pencils
- Project Book page 47
- Students' containers with fruits or vegetables

Ask groups to observe what is happening to the object of their experiment. Have them color the items in the second column according to what they see in each container (in the order their containers are placed).
When students finish, have them put their materials away and say *goodbye* to their classmates and to you.

Unit 6

WHICH CONTAINER CAN'T YOU USE TO PUT RAVIOLI IN THE FREEZER? CROSS IT OUT.

STEAM • WHY IS FOOD IMPORTANT? • UNIT 6 49

Learning goals
- Use play dough to make fruit
- Classify food containers according to what they can store, liquids or non-liquids
- Analyze containers to store ravioli in a freezer and think of ways to transform a bottle into a ravioli container

STEAM subjects
- Science
- Engineering
- Arts
- Math

Thinking skills
Remembering, understanding, applying, creating, analyzing, evaluating, improving

Main language content
Cut the bottle. Cover the bottle.
It's liquid. It isn't liquid.
Food items: *apple, banana, pasta, potato, ravioli, spaghetti*
Food containers: *bottle, jar, plastic bag*

OPENING

Circle time

Materials and preparation
- A bell
- Puppet
- Visual schedule pictures

Say *hello* to students and invite them to sit in a circle. Encourage them to say *hello* to you and the puppet. Make it answer, *Hello, my friends.*
Then place the visual schedule pictures face down in the circle. Call on a student to turn over a picture and show it to the rest of the class. Elicit the name of the subject. Invite a student to make the bell chime and ask, *Can you hear the chime?* Elicit from the rest of the class, *It's (engineering) time!* Repeat with the other subjects.

Science and arts – Make play dough fruits and vegetables.

Materials and preparation
- Play dough

Have students make play dough apples, bananas, and potatoes. Ask, *Do you remember the color of fruits and vegetables when they are oxidizing? Can you make them look oxidized?* Have them first make a fruit or vegetable using brown play dough.

> **Note to teachers**
> Make some time in today's class to have students check the progress of their oxidation experiment and record it under the column named *THE NEXT DAY*.

52 STEAM

ACTIVE LEARNING

Science and math – Understand food packaging.

Materials and preparation
- Bottle (plastic or aluminum)
- Box of cookies or cereal
- Freezer bag
- Jar
- Milk carton
- Snack box

Show students each of the containers, say the word for it, and ask, *Is this for food or drinks? What food/drink can you put here?* Elicit ideas and make sure students are always encouraged to participate, even if it is by guessing.
Then have students classify the items into containers for liquids (bottle, jar, and carton) and for non-liquids. Ask, *How many for liquids? How many for non-liquids?*

Engineering and math – Which container can't you use to put ravioli in the freezer? Cross it out.

Materials and preparation
- Pencils
- Project Book page 49

Have students open their Project Book to page 49. Show them the picture in the middle and ask, *What is this kind of pasta called?* See if students recognize it as ravioli or teach them the name. Then help them name the containers around the ravioli. Say, *This ravioli needs to go to the freezer.* *Can you put it in a (freezer bag)?* Ask about the other containers. Keep in mind that students might not be familiar with the possibility of using the containers for ravioli, so help them think about the size of the ravioli and the size of the container and say whether it fits in the container. Say, *Yes, some people store pasta in a freezer bag.* When you talk about the plastic bottle, ask the question and make sure students realize that ravioli wouldn't get into the bottle because of its size. Tell students to cross out that food container and say what they could store in a bottle (milk, water, juice, etc.).

DIFFERENTIATED INSTRUCTION

BELOW LEVEL
Engineering – Find a way to make ravioli get into the bottle.

Materials and preparation
- A large plastic lid
- A plastic bottle
- Aluminum foil paper
- Freezer bag
- Scissors or knife (teacher use only)
- Small bows (to represent the ravioli)
- Tape

Tell students that you are going to eat ravioli and you only have a plastic bottle with you. Ask, *How can I put the ravioli into the bottle to put in the freezer?* Allow students to come up with ideas, such as cut the ravioli in small pieces or make a large hole in the bottle. If no one mentions removing the upper part of the bottle, suggest it yourself.
Cut the bottle in half and invite someone to place the bows in it – make sure they fit into the bottle. Say, *Great! But I still have a problem. How can I cover the ravioli?* Turn the bottle over and make the "ravioli" fall so as to show the problem. Show students the materials they can use to make a cap and have them work in small groups. They can use the materials to cover and tape to hold the cover. They can't use the large lid as it is too large for the container.

ABOVE LEVEL

Have students follow the procedures explained in *Below level*, but after asking how you can cover the ravioli, don't show students any materials and have them come up with suggestions of materials themselves. Have them test their suggestions and show their classmates if they worked out. Encourage their classmates to think of solutions to make all ideas work somehow.

Note to teachers
Make sure to challenge students so as to make them think of the question, propose a solution, test it, analyze the results, and improve their solution. This way they will be developing basic engineering skills.

CLOSING

Sing *Eat fruits*. Say goodbye.

Materials and preparation
- Audio library – songs
- Puppet

Have students sit in a circle. Play the song *Eat fruits* (track 14) and tell students to clap every time they hear the name of some fruit or vegetable. Play the song again and have them sing and dance together with the puppet.
Then say *goodbye* to students and encourage them to reply.

Learning goals
- Check statements about food
- Get introduced to the concept of conditional for running a program
- Categorize food items into hot and cold
- Learn to think of and test hypotheses by answering *What if* questions

STEAM subjects
- Science
- Technology
- Engineering
- Arts
- Math

Thinking skills
Remembering, understanding, applying, creating, analyzing

Main language content
If it is red, it's true.
Is it true? Is it false?
Or else…?
What if oranges weren't orange?
Food: *apple, ice cream, orange, potato, spaghetti, tomato*

OPENING

Circle time
Materials and preparation
- A bell
- A book
- Puppet
- Visual schedule pictures

Say *hello* to students. Encourage them to say *hello* to you and the puppet. Make it answer, *Hello, my friends.*
Cover the pictures of today's schedule using a book. Hold the pictures behind the book and show part of them only. Ask students if they can guess what activity it is. Repeat with the other picture.
Show one picture at a time, invite a student to make the bell chime, and help them to ask, *Can you hear the chime?*
Elicit from the others, *It's (arts) time!* Repeat with the other subjects.

Math – What's missing?
Materials and preparation
- Props or real food items in packages (you can also use pictures)

Place the food items or props in the circle and ask students to take a good look. Call one student up and have the rest stand up and turn around. The student called removes one of the items and the others have to remember which item is missing. Ask, *What is missing?* and have students try to recall the items they saw. Start with fewer items (three) and then add more as you see students understand the game.
Play a few times and have different students remove the items. Remove more than one item at a time and ask, *How many items then? How many items now? How many missing items?*

STEAM

ACTIVE LEARNING

Science and technology – Check food statements and learn about conditions.

Materials and preparation
- Flashcards: *apple, ice cream, orange, potato, tomato*
- Pencils
- Sheets of paper (one per student)

Distribute the sheets of paper and pencils. Tell students that you are going to show them a food flashcard and say a statement. Explain to the students that they will have to choose if the statement is true or false and you will give them the options of what to do if the statement is true.
Start by saying the following statement: *All apples are red. If it is true, then draw red apples. Else, draw other colors.* Put special emphasis on the words *if*, *then*, and *else*. Suggested statements: *Ice cream is hot. Orange is the name of a fruit and a color. Potato is a vegetable. Tomatoes are healthy.* Have students compare their drawings and see if they considered the same things true.

> **Note to teachers**
> When working with *if*, *then*, and *else* statements students get introduced to the concept of designing a computer program with specific information and to making decisions based on the information it knows to be true.

Science and math – Which food do you usually eat cold? Circle them blue.

Materials and preparation
- Pencils
- Project Book page 51

Have students open their Project Book to page 51. Show them the pictures and ask, *Do you eat ice cream hot or cold?* As students answer, have them identify that ice cream is cold – help them understand the meaning of the word *ice*. Tell them to circle the ice cream blue. Then have students identify the other food items that are cold. When they finish, have them compare the items and say which food items are cold and hot.

DIFFERENTIATED INSTRUCTION

BELOW LEVEL
Engineering and arts – Create hypothetical food.

Materials and preparation
- Flashcards: *apple, ice cream, orange, potato, tomato*
- Play dough

Give students some play dough and divide them into five groups. Assign a flashcard to each group and elicit the name of the food items. Ask them hypothetical questions and have them use play dough to design the food as you say. Say to the ice cream group, *What if ice cream was a fruit?* And have students discuss with their group a possibility: maybe it could be a creamy strawberry, maybe it could be sugar-free, etc. Allow students to be creative and design their ideas as they want. Suggested sentences for the other groups: *What if apples were rectangular? What if oranges were blue? What if potatoes were sweet? What if tomatoes had hair?*

ABOVE LEVEL
Divide students into the same food groups and give them the same material as explained in *Below level*, but raise questions that can allow students to use their imagination even more, such as: *What if apples weren't round? What if ice cream wasn't cold? What if oranges were another color? What if potatoes looked ugly? What if tomatoes weren't round?*

CLOSING

Talk about meals. Sing *The meals song*. Say goodbye.

Materials and preparation
- Audio library – songs

Ask students to say what they usually eat for breakfast, lunch, snack, and dinner. Have them compare if they have similar tastes in food.
Play *The meals song* (track 15) and have students sing along and dance. After the song, say *goodbye* to students and encourage them to say *goodbye* to each other.

Unit 7 How can farm animals help us?

Learning goals
- Learn about the life cycle of a chicken and make a craft
- Suggest improvements for the craft
- Compare shapes and sizes to a chick's body
- Decipher a code to make part of a robot chick

STEAM subjects
- Science
- Technology
- Engineering
- Arts
- Math

Thinking skills
Conceptualizing, applying, analyzing, creating, evaluating

Main language content
It's an egg. It's a hatching egg. It's a chick.
It's a chicken.
The head is a big circle. The beak is a small triangle.
Chicken life cycle: *chick, chicken, egg, hatching egg*
Shapes: *circle, half a circle, triangle*
Sizes: *big, small*

OPENING

Circle time

Materials and preparation
- A bell
- Puppet
- Visual schedule pictures

Say *hello* to students and invite them to sit in a circle. Encourage them to say *hello* to you and the puppet. Make it answer, *Hello, my friends.*
Then place the visual schedule pictures face down in the circle. Call on a student to turn over a picture and show it to the rest of the class. Elicit the name of the subject. Invite a student to make the bell chime and ask, *Can you hear the chime?* Elicit from the rest of the class, *It's (engineering) time!* Repeat with the other subjects.

Science and math – Chicken life cycle

Materials and preparation
- Masking tape
- Pictures of the life cycle of a chicken: an egg, an egg hatching with a chick in it, a little chick, a chicken

Have students remain sitting in a circle. Place the four pictures in the middle of the circle in random order and ask students what they see in each of the pictures. Then say, *This is the chicken's life cycle. What happens first?* Have students discuss for a while and call on a volunteer to use masking tape to place the egg picture on the wall. Ask, *What happens next?* After some discussion, ask another student to place that picture next to the other. Go on until the four pictures are side by side on the wall. Leave them there for the closing activity.

ACTIVE LEARNING

Arts, engineering, and math – Make a craft chick out of shapes.

Materials and preparation
- Big yellow circle cutouts (one per student)
- Glue
- Markers
- Small orange triangle cutouts (one per student)
- Small yellow circle cutouts (one per student)

Distribute the materials to students and tell them that they are going to make a chick. Have them first name the shapes they can see. Then say, *Let's use a big yellow circle and a small yellow circle and a small orange triangle to make a chick. How can you make the chick?* Have students discuss with a classmate ways they can put the shapes together to form a chick. Allow them to test possibilities before gluing the parts together. Tell them to think about which of the shapes represents the chick's head and draw eyes on it.

When they finish, ask them to show their classmates their chicks and compare if they used the same shapes for the same purposes: *Which one is the chick's head, the small or big circle?*

Arts and engineering – Make your chick better.

Materials and preparation
- Paper bags
- Play dough
- Students' craft chick
- Wooden clothespins (two per student)

Show students the materials and say, *Our chick is not complete. What's missing?* Elicit, *The legs.* Ask how many legs a chick has and elicit the answer. Show students the clothespins and have them think of ways they can use the clothespins to make legs (they can put the clothespins in some flattened play dough so that it works as the basis of the "legs").
When they finish, tell them to try to make the chick stand. Ask those whose chicken can't stand how they can solve this. Allow the others to participate as well. Then give them play dough and let them work. If they can't solve it by themselves, tell them to try making a thick layer of play dough to place around the clothespins as if it were the ground. When a student manages to do this, have them show their solution to the other classmates.

> **Note to teachers**
> Some of the students' crafts may stand without the need of play dough. If that is the case, have those students help the ones whose chick can't stand without play dough.

DIFFERENTIATED INSTRUCTION

BELOW LEVEL
Technology and math – Connect the shapes to make wings on the robot chick. What's the code?

Materials and preparation
- Pencils
- Project Book page 53

Have students open their Project Book to page 53. Show them the robot and ask, *What animal is it?* Elicit, *A chick.* Point to the missing wing and tell students to connect the shapes with a line and find out what part of the chick's body it is.
When they finish, elicit the word *wing* and ask how many wings a chick has. Ask students what shapes they see in the wing and say, *There is sequence in this wing. This sequence is a code. Say the shapes with me: circle, circle, triangle, circle, circle, triangle.* Have students identify that the code is two circles and a triangle one after the other.

ABOVE LEVEL
Do the procedures explained in *Below level*, but instead of having students say the shapes and the sequence with you, just tell them that there is a code hidden in the wing and have them talk to a classmate and try to discover the code. Then elicit the sequence and have them find out the code.

CLOSING

Play *Tap the pictures*. Say goodbye.

Materials and preparation
- Pictures students placed on the wall in the opening activity

Have students line up in front of the pictures. Say a stage of the life cycle of a chicken and have the first student in line run and tap it. Play the game twice; the first time you play say the stages randomly, but the second time, have students run to the picture, tap it, and say the stages in order. Then ask for students' help to collect the pictures and clean up. Say *goodbye* to all of them and have them say *goodbye* to you.

Learning goals
- Identify farm animals and their houses
- Design, plan, and build a chicken coop
- Learn to calculate how many items are missing in a group

STEAM subjects
- Science
- Engineering
- Arts
- Math

Thinking skills
Remembering, understanding, applying, analyzing, creating, evaluating

Main language content
It's a big coop. Where do chickens live?
How many hatched eggs?
Farm animals and their houses: *chick, chicken, coop, horse, stable*
Numbers: 1-7
Shapes: *circle (round), oval, triangle*

OPENING

Circle time

Materials and preparation
- A bell
- Visual schedule pictures

Have all the students sit in a circle. Greet them and invite them to greet you back. Review the procedures for gathering in a circle. Hide the pictures representing today's schedule and have students look for them. Then place them in the circle.
Call on a student to be the class helper and give the bell to them. Have them make the bell chime and ask, *Can you hear the chime?* Ask students if they remember how to reply and help as needed. Show a picture of one of today's activities and elicit, *It's (science) time!* Repeat with the other subjects.

Play a memory game.

Materials and preparation
- Pictures glued on construction paper cut into squares: a chicken, a chicken coop, a horse, a stable

Have students remain sitting in a circle. Place the pictures facing down in the middle of the circle. Have one student at a time turn over two pictures and tell you the words they know. Teach them the words for the animal houses. If they find a pair, have them leave it facing up in the circle until all pictures are facing up. Ask students if they have ever visited these places where farm animals stay and tell the group about their experience.

ACTIVE LEARNING

Engineering and arts – Plan and design a chicken coop.

Materials and preparation
- Cardboard boxes
- Pencils
- Picture of a coop
- Play dough
- Popsicle sticks
- Scraps of paper
- Sheets of paper
- Students' chick crafts from previous class

Ask students to say again where chickens live as you show them the picture. Then ask, *Do you remember the chicks we made last class? They don't have a shelter! What can we do?*
Ask students to think of ways they could build a coop. Let them brainstorm ideas and suggest materials. If you have any other materials available, let students use them. Then show all the material you have available and have students work in small groups. Give them paper and pencil to make a plan. Move your hands vertically and horizontally as you ask, *Is your coop vertical or horizontal?* Give them time to work.
Then have groups present what they have made. Encourage them to talk about the materials they have used and test how many chicks can live in the coop.

> **Note to teachers**
> As students may not be familiar yet with the concept of vertical and horizontal, make sure to gesture so as to make them understand the directions you are referring to.

Science and math – Look and count. How many chicks are missing? Draw.

Materials and preparation
- Colored pencils
- Project Book page 55

Ask students if they remember the chicken life cycle and help them retell it. Have them open their Project Book to page 55 and tell you what part of the life cycle each line of pictures represents. Then tell students, *Look! Eggs! How many eggs?* Elicit *Seven!* Ask, *How many hatched eggs?* Elicit *Seven!* Then point to the chicks and have them count. Say, *Wait, seven eggs, but only five chicks? Where are the other chicks?* Ask students how many chicks are missing and have them draw two chicks more.

DIFFERENTIATED INSTRUCTION

BELOW LEVEL
Science – Play *Human chicks*.

Materials and preparation
- Camera (optional)

Divide students into groups of four. If you don't have an even number, invite a fast-finisher to join two groups, one after they have finished helping the other. Have students work together to make a human chick. They will lie on the floor as you tell them to. One student will lie down on their side and pretend to be the chick's head, holding their arms open as if they were scissors (this will be the beak). Have another student lie down near the first student's feet to be the body; then have two more students pretend to be the feet. Invite students to watch their classmates or take pictures of groups to show everyone.

ABOVE LEVEL
Have students work in groups of four as well and try to make a human chick lying on the floor as explained in *Below level*. However, don't tell students how to form the chick. Just remind them of the chick's body parts and have them figure out how to make the chick by themselves. Ask questions to help students organize themselves: *Where is the beak? Hey, "head", can you make a beak with your arms?*

CLOSING

Science – Play *Broken telephone* using animal sounds.

Have students sit in a circle and ask a student to whisper a farm animal sound to the next student. The next student does the same with whoever is sitting next to him. The last student has to make the animal sound they were told and also say what animal makes that sound. Have the student who started the activity check if the animal and the sound are correct. After playing the game a few times more, have students clean-up and wave goodbye.

WHAT ANIMALS ARE MISSING? FOLLOW THE SEQUENCE OF THE SONG AND DRAW.

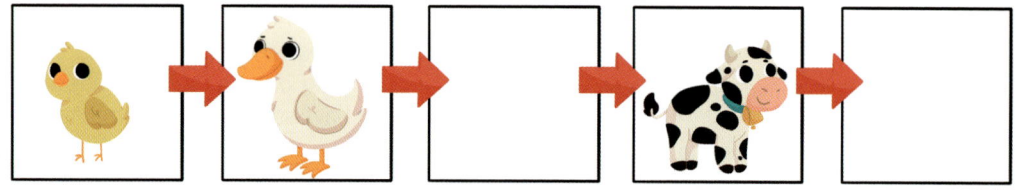

STEAM • HOW CAN FARM ANIMALS HELP US? • UNIT 7   57

Learning goals
- Group farm animals
- Make a graph and compare the number of animals in a farm
- Make a sheep mask

STEAM subjects
- Arts
- Math

Thinking skills
Remembering, understanding, applying, analyzing, creating

Main language content
How many animals?
Three.
Farm animals: *cow, donkey, duck, horse, sheep*
Comparative adjectives: *higher, lower*
Numbers: *1-32*

OPENING

Circle time
Materials and preparation
- A bell
- A book
- Puppet
- Visual schedule pictures

Say *hello* to students. Encourage them to say *hello* to you and the puppet. Make it answer, *Hello, my friends.*
Cover the pictures of today's schedule using a book. Hold the pictures behind the book and show part of them only. Ask students if they can guess what activity it is. Repeat with the other picture.
Show one picture at a time, invite a student to make the bell chime, and help them to ask, *Can you hear the chime?*
Elicit from the others, *It's (arts) time!* Repeat with the other subject.

Math – Find and count the pictures.
Materials and preparation
- Eight pieces of string
- Eight pictures of a cow
- Eight pictures of a donkey
- Eight pictures of a duck
- Eight pictures of a horse

Make eight sets of pictures, each set containing a different animal card, and use string to tie the four pictures together. Before class, hide them around the classroom.
Have students look for the sets of pictures. When they find the sets, have them bring the pictures back to the circle and help you spread them all. Ask, *How many pictures in a set? How many different animals can you see?*
Then have students count all the animals in the cards. Ask, *How many cows?* and elicit *Eight*. Then ask, *How many animals in all?* Have students rote count to thirty-two as you point to the animals.

60 STEAM

ACTIVE LEARNING

Arts and math – What animals are missing? Follow the sequence of the song and draw.

Materials and preparation
- Audio library – songs
- Pencils
- Project Book page 57

Play the song *Old MacDonald* (track 16) and have students dance and sing. Next, have students open their Project Book to page 57 and say the animals they see. Tell them to look at the boxes. Ask, *What is missing in the boxes?* Help them understand that they have a group of animals there, so two animals are missing. Explain that you will play the song again and they will point to the animals as they hear them. When they don't hear an animal, they will draw it to complete the sequence of the song.
Play the song as many times as necessary, giving them time to draw each of the animals. Then have students tell you the sequence of animals in the song.

Math – Make a graph about animals on a farm.

Materials and preparation
- A large piece of poster paper (two pieces if you have a large group)
- Glue
- Markers
- Ten pictures of a cow
- Ten pictures of a duck
- Ten pictures of a horse

Draw a cow, a duck, and a horse at the bottom of the poster, or use printed pictures and glue, so that students can use the animals as the starting point for a graph. Meanwhile, place all the pictures together and have students group the animals in the pictures, placing all cows on one table, all ducks on another, and all horses on a third table.
Tell students that they are going to listen to a story about a farm and they need to help you organize the farm. This way, they will be making a bar graph. Say, *This is a big farm. It has lots of animals. It has four cows.* Call out four students to glue the cow pictures one above the other in the cow column. Help them as needed.
Then tell students, *This farm also has five ducks and seven horses.* Have a group of students select five out of the ten duck pictures and another group select seven out of the ten horses. Ask them to glue the pictures in the correct column. Finally tell them to count again and say how many of each animal they can see.

DIFFERENTIATED INSTRUCTION

BELOW LEVEL
Math – Compare the number of animals.

Materials and preparation
- Farm animals graph from previous activity
- Masking ape

Use tape to display the poster showing the graph on the wall so that everyone can see it. Have students work in pairs and ask them questions to help them compare the data in the graph: *How many cows? How many horses? Which number is higher, five or seven? Which bar goes higher?* As you use the word *higher*, gesture so that students understand what it means.
Ask them more questions, comparing other animals and using the word *lower*, too.

ABOVE LEVEL

Divide students into pairs and have them look at the graph as explained in *Below level*, but instead of asking them questions, have pairs talk about the information and count the animals by themselves. Then have them say the difference between the number of horses and ducks, for example: *Seven horses and five ducks. There are more horses, two more.*

CLOSING

Play *Old MacDonald*. Say goodbye.

Materials and preparation
- Audio library – songs

Have students stand up and divide them into five groups. Assign each group a farm animal. Tell them they can only start dancing when they hear their animal in the song. Play the song *Old MacDonald* (track 16). As the song ends, all animals will be dancing in the farm.
After the song, ask students to help you tidy up. Then say *goodbye* to them and have them say *goodbye* to you.

MAKE COLORFUL SHEEP WOOL.

STEAM • HOW CAN FARM ANIMALS HELP US? • UNIT 7 • 59

Learning goals
- Learn about estimation
- Find out what animal products can help them
- Learn about texture and make a colorful sheep

STEAM subjects
- Science
- Arts
- Math

Thinking skills

Remembering, understanding, applying, analyzing, creating

Main language content

What product is soft?
This is my sheep. The wool is yellow.
Animal products: *egg, milk, wool*
Colors: *black, blue, brown, green, orange, pink, purple, red, yellow, white*
Numbers: *1-35*

OPENING

Circle time

Materials and preparation
- A bell
- A book
- Puppet
- Visual schedule pictures

Say *hello* to students. Encourage them to say *hello* to you and the puppet. Make it answer, *Hello, my friends.*
Cover the pictures of today's schedule using a book. Hold the pictures behind the book and show part of them only. Ask students if they can guess what activity it is. Repeat with the other picture.
Show one picture at a time, invite a student to make the bell chime, and help them to ask, *Can you hear the chime?*
Elicit from the others, *It's (arts) time!* Repeat with the other subjects.

Science – What products do animals give us?

Materials and preparation
- An empty carton of milk (or a closed one)
- An egg
- Wool

Have students remain in a circle. Show them the three animal products and have students pass them around in the circle to find out what they are. Then place the pictures on three separate desks in the classroom and invite students to stay between the three tables. Ask, *What does a cow give us?* Tell students to run to the desk where the milk is. Ask more questions about the other animal products. You can also call a student to ask the questions.

ACTIVE LEARNING

Math – Estimating pompoms in a jar

Materials and preparation
- A jar
- About 30 pompoms

Show the pompoms and have students touch them. Ask, *What animal product is similar to this? What product is soft?* Have them feel the texture and elicit *Wool*. Ask, *What animal gives us wool?* Encourage students to answer and imitate a sheep by going *baa*.
Place all the pompoms in a jar or have students help you do it. Ask, *How many pompoms in here? Can you guess?* As students guess, gesture with your hand up and down as you give them the clues *more* or *less*.
Allow everyone to make a guess. You can also have them count the pompoms.

Science and arts – Make colorful sheep wool.

Materials and preparation
- Cotton balls (a few per student)
- Glue
- Pompoms (a few per student)
- Project Book page 59

Have students open their Project Book to page 59. Have them look at the sheep and elicit the name of the animal. Say, *Let's make the wool to glue on the sheep.*

How about we make colorful wool? Tell students they can't use colored pencils, crayons, or markers. Allow them to give some suggestions. If anyone mentions pompoms, show them the materials available.
Have students glue some white cotton and some colored pompoms on the sheep. Then tell them to show their work to a classmate and say, *This is my sheep. The wool is (white, black, and yellow).*

DIFFERENTIATED INSTRUCTION

BELOW LEVEL
Math – Group sheep according to color.

Materials and preparation
- Students' sheep

Have students show each other the sheep and see if they find similar colors in their classmates' sheep. Tell them to group the sheep according to the colors they used. If three of them have blue pompoms, even though they have other colors, they can stay in the same group.
Make sure all sheep are grouped at the end of the activity. Then have students explain the predominant color in a group and count how many there are in each group.

ABOVE LEVEL
Math – Group sheep according to color and number of pompoms.

Materials and preparation
- Students' sheep

After students have done the procedures explained in *Below level*, have them also count how many colored pompoms they used and compare with their classmates. If they find classmates with the same number of colored pompoms, have them stay in a group. When all groups are formed, have students count how many sheep there are in each group.

CLOSING

Tell the puppet what you know. Say goodbye.

Materials and preparation
- Puppet

Have students sit in a circle. Say, *(Puppet's name) can't remember much of our classes. Can you help? Tell the puppet what you learned about farm animals.* Have students say the names of the animals, the products they can provide, and where some farm animals stay.
Allow them to say what their favorite part of the last classes was and say *goodbye* to each one of them individually. Have them say *goodbye* to you and the puppet.

Unit 8 Who lives and works in my town?

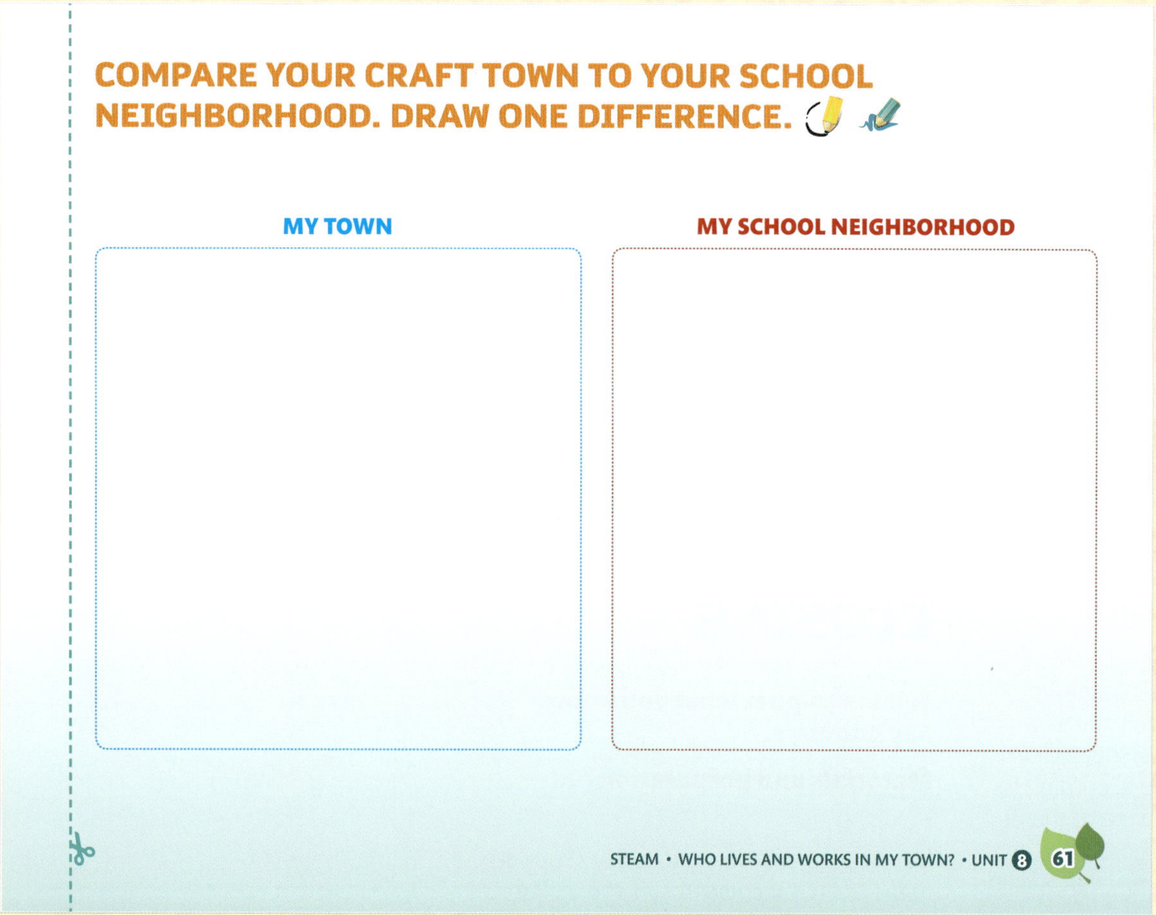

COMPARE YOUR CRAFT TOWN TO YOUR SCHOOL NEIGHBORHOOD. DRAW ONE DIFFERENCE.

MY TOWN

MY SCHOOL NEIGHBORHOOD

STEAM • WHO LIVES AND WORKS IN MY TOWN? • UNIT 8 61

OPENING

Circle time

Materials and preparation
- A bell
- A book
- Puppet
- Visual schedule pictures

Say *hello* to students. Encourage them to say *hello* to you and the puppet. Make it answer, *Hello, my friends*.
Cover the pictures of today's schedule using a book. Hold the pictures behind the book and show part of them only. Ask students if they can guess what activity it is. Repeat with the other picture. Show one picture at a time, invite a student to make the bell chime, and help them to ask, *Can you hear the chime?*
Elicit from the others, *It's (engineering) time!* Repeat with the other subjects.

Talk about your neighborhood.

Ask students, *Do you know the name of your street? What color is your house or apartment building? Are there many trees in your neighborhood? Can you name one store close to your home?* Allow students time to think and talk. Encourage everyone to share what they know about their neighborhood.

Learning goals
- Work on spatial concepts and the concept of urban planning
- Make a town model

STEAM subjects
- Science
- Engineering
- Arts
- Math

Thinking skills
Remembering, understanding, applying, analyzing, creating, evaluating

Main language content
How many houses are there?
There is a park.
Places in town: *bakery, park, restaurant, school*

STEAM

ACTIVE LEARNING

Engineering and arts – Make your home for the town.

Materials and preparation
- Construction paper
- Glue
- Large pieces of cardboard
- Markers
- Medicine boxes
- Paint
- Sponges

Cut the sponges into small rectangles. Tell students that today you are going to make a town.
Give students a small medicine box and tell them that it represents their house. Ask, *How can you make it look like your home?* Have students use a piece of sponge to color the box according to the color of their house. Have them show their house to a classmate and talk about it.

Engineering and arts – Make other places in town for your town.

Materials and preparation
- Glue
- Green paper
- Medicine boxes
- Paint
- Play dough
- Popsicle sticks
- Students' town

Divide students into groups and give each a piece of cardboard and glue. Ask, *How do cars go around this town?* Help students understand that they need streets in their town. Help them make the lines to represent streets. Then ask, *Are there only houses in a town? What else is there?* Elicit names of places in a town and give the group a few more boxes for them to make these places as well.
Allow students to be creative and think of ways they can improve their town, such as by making a park with green paper and trees using green circles and popsicle sticks on play dough.
Invite groups to present their work to their classmates and say what there is in their town and how many houses there are.

Note to teachers
Make sure you encourage students to imagine, create, improve, and reflect on their work.

DIFFERENTIATED INSTRUCTION

BELOW LEVEL
Arts and math – Compare your craft town to your school neighborhood. Draw one difference.

Materials and preparation
- Colored pencils
- Project Book page 61

Ask students to sit in a circle with their group and say how similar and different their craft town is from the school neighborhood. Elicit the discussion by asking, *Are there trees in the school neighborhood? Is there a restaurant? Are houses (blue and green), too?*
Have students open their Project Book to page 61 and draw one difference between their school neighborhood and their craft town. Give them examples such as, *One has lots of houses, the other just a few. One has a park, the other has a restaurant.*

ABOVE LEVEL
Have students look at another group's craft town and compare it to the school neighborhood. Only ask questions if necessary. You can also tell them what to talk about without asking questions, if necessary. Say, for instance, *Talk about the number and color of the houses, the shapes in them, the trees and other places.*
After that, have them do the activity in their Project Book page 61 the same way as explained in *Below level*.

CLOSING

Arts – An exhibit in my school

Materials and preparation
- Students' craft towns

Choose a place in the school for students to place their craft towns. If possible, invite students and school staff to visit the exhibit. Have students present the things in their town.
Leave the craft towns in that area for a few days and encourage students to invite other people to visit, such as their parents or friends outside the school.
Take students back to the classroom, ask them to clean up, and say *goodbye* to them.

Note to teachers
Students develop their spatial awareness when relating objects to their own environment.

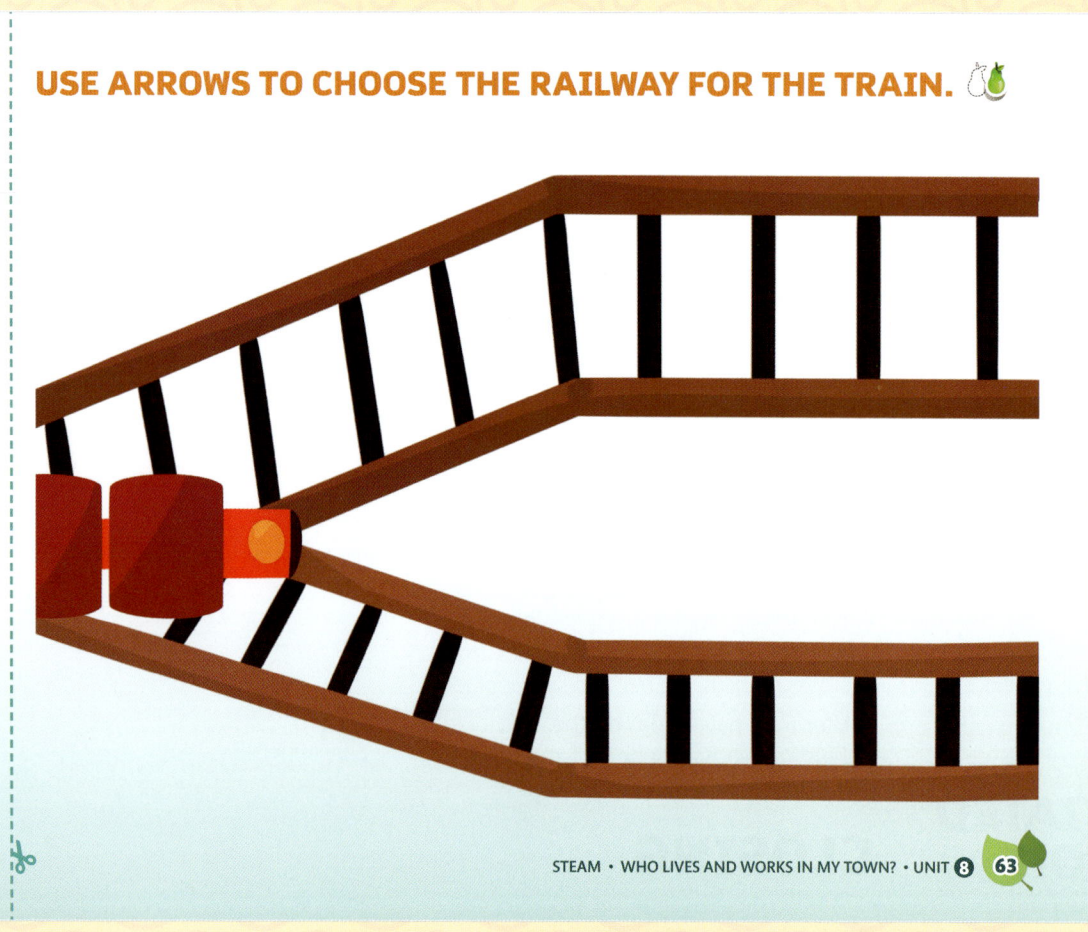

Learning goals
- Learn about magnetism by making a train move
- Use role-playing to learn about trains
- Develop a program with an algorithm for a railway involving branching (decisions)
- Measure and compare the width of a train and railways

STEAM subjects
- Science
- Technology
- Engineering
- Arts
- Math

Thinking skills
Remembering, understanding, applying, analyzing, creating

Main language content
It's a train. It has eight wagons.
Go up the hill. Go down the hill.
It's wider. It's just right.
Numbers: *1-20*

OPENING

Circle time

Materials and preparation
- A bell
- Visual schedule pictures

Have all the students sit in a circle, facing you. Greet them and invite them to greet you back. Review the procedures for gathering in a circle.
Hide the pictures representing today's schedule and have students look for them. Then place them in the circle.
Call on a student to be the class helper and give the bell to them. Have them make the bell chime and ask, *Can you hear the chime?* Ask students if they remember how to reply and help as needed. Show a picture of one of today's activities and elicit, *It's (technology) time!* Repeat with the other subjects.

Arts and math – Role-play the wagon journey

Ask students, *Where would you go if you could travel on a train today?* Tell students that in this game they are going to be the wagons of a train. Choose one student to be the engine and have the student go around the classroom making train noises. Then they back up into another student who grabs onto their waist, this way connecting like a wagon to the engine. After that, tell them to go *choo* around the classroom until they back up onto another student, who then grabs into the last wagon's waist and connects their wagon to the train. Continue until all students are part of the train.
When a student becomes part of the train, have the other students count how many wagons there are.

ACTIVE LEARNING

Science – Use magnets to make a train move.

Materials and preparation
- Magnets
- Poster board
- Tape
- Train engine cutouts

Display the poster board and ask for students' help to draw some paths, a very common scenery to see trains in. Have a student use tape to attach a magnet to the back of the train engine cutout. Invite another student to hold a magnet behind the poster board and have them move the engine around, up and down the hills, as their classmates tell them to: *Go up the hill. Go down the hill.* Model first; then have different students hold the train. Explain that the train moves because one magnet is attracting the other magnet.

Technology, engineering, and math – Use arrows to choose the railway for the train.

Materials and preparation
- Popsicle sticks
- Project Book page 63
- Unit 8 Stickers

Have students open their Project Book to page 63. Point to the train and elicit the word. Point to the railways and say, *This train has two railways ahead of it, but it can only follow one.* Give students popsicle sticks to measure the width of the train and the railways and say which railway is as wide as the train.

When students have found this information, have them peel off the stickers of Unit 8 and place the arrows so as to show the path the train should follow.

Check students' work and make sure they are sticking the arrows pointing to the right side.

> **Note to teachers**
> Branching is an instruction that tells a computer to begin executing a different part of a program. When students need to make decisions about the train path, they are getting introduced to branching.

DIFFERENTIATED INSTRUCTION

BELOW LEVEL
Math – Find a shape that is as wide as the other railway.

Materials and preparation
- Rectangle cutouts (three per pair of students, one of them as wide as the first railway on page 63)
- Project Book page 63

Divide students into pairs. Give each pair of students a few shapes. Tell them that they will find out how wide the train that goes on the other railway is. Have students work together to measure the shapes on the railway. When they find out what shape has the same width, check their choices and encourage them to keep trying if they didn't get the right shape.

ABOVE LEVEL
Math – Cut out a shape that is as wide as the other railway.

Materials and preparation
- Construction paper (half a sheet per student)
- Project Book page 63
- Scissors

Have students work in pairs. Give them a piece of construction paper and tell them to try to cut a piece that is as large as the train that will go on the other railway, the first track. Have other pairs of students check their classmates' cutout and measure with the track to see if the train can run on the track.

CLOSING

Play *Don't step on the track.* Say goodbye.

Invite six students to be the track. Have them lie on the floor forming two lines as far from each other as the average height of students. Have two other students lie down between the two lines, thus forming a short track.

Invite the other students to line up in front of the "track" and pretend to be trains running on the track. Remind them to be careful so as not to step on any classmates. Have them make a train sound and remind them that they can't step on the track, but in between parts of the track. Have all students pretend to be trains and invite other students to form a track. Then say *goodbye* to students and have them say *goodbye* to you.

LOOK AND SAY. WHAT'S MISSING? GLUE.

MAKE A BEAUTIFUL GARDEN FOR THE HOUSE.

Learning goals
- Learn about the things they do at different places in a town
- Reflect on essential parts of a house
- Make the roof of a house and decorate its garden

STEAM subjects
- Engineering
- Arts

Thinking skills
Remembering, understanding, applying, analyzing, creating

Main language content
What color is your house? What are the parts of a house?
Places in town: *apartment building, house, park, restaurant, school, supermarket*
Activities: *buy food, ride a bike, study*

OPENING

Circle time
Materials and preparation
- A bell
- Puppet
- Visual schedule pictures

Bring out the puppet and start by having it greet the students. After they greet the puppet, have the puppet greet you, too. Then elicit *Hello!* and ask students how they are today.
Hide the pictures representing today's schedule and have students look for them. Then place them in the circle. Use the attention-getter to introduce today's schedule. Make the bell chime and ask, *Can you hear the chime?* Ask students if they remember how to reply and help as needed.
Show a picture of one of today's activities and elicit, *It's (arts) time!* Repeat with the other subject.

Where do you…?
Materials and preparation
- Masking tape
- Pictures of an apartment building, house, park, restaurant, school, and a supermarket

Place the pictures one across from the other on the wall in the classroom, having half of them on one side and half on the other. Tell students to run to the correct picture according to what they do there. Say, for instance, *Buy food, ride a bike, study.* Keep in mind that students' answers may vary.

ACTIVE LEARNING

Engineering and arts - Look and say. What's missing? Glue.

Materials and preparation
- Glue
- Play dough
- Popsicle sticks
- Project Book page 65
- Roof-shaped pieces of paper (triangles)

Have students open their Project Book to page 65. Ask, *What can you see? How many rooms are there in this house? Can you name the rooms?*
Tell students that something is missing in this house. Allow them to figure out what is missing. If necessary, point to the roof area and say that something is missing there. After they have figured out that the roof is missing, let them choose from the materials available what to use to make the roof: popsicle sticks, play dough, or roof-shaped pieces of paper.
Have students compare their roof with a classmate's and say if it is the same or different.

Arts - Make a beautiful garden for the house.

Materials and preparation
- Colored markers
- Crayons
- Glue
- Pieces of green crepe paper

When students have finished their roofs, show them the bottom part of the house. Say, *Something is missing here, too... What is it?* If needed, give clues such as, *It's green. It's beautiful.* Have students make their gardens using the materials available in the way they choose.

DIFFERENTIATED INSTRUCTION

BELOW LEVEL
Compare your roofs and gardens.

Materials and preparation
- Students' house project

Have students work in pairs. Tell them to take turns telling each other about what they used for the roof and for the garden in their house. Then ask pairs, *Are they the same? What is similar?*

ABOVE LEVEL

Have students look for classmates who used the same material as themselves to make the roof of the house and stay together in a group. In case there are large groups, divide them into two subgroups. Tell them to talk about any other similarities they can find in their roof and garden and to talk about the differences, too.

CLOSING

Talk about the color of your bedroom and sing the *Goodbye song*.

Materials and preparation
- Audio library - songs

Play the *Goodbye song* (track 03) while students walk around the classroom. As you pause the song, have students stop in front of a classmate and say the color of their bedroom. If the color is the same, they can sit down. If not, they will continue to walk as you play the song again. Play it a few more times before saying *goodbye* to students.

> **Note to teachers**
> When you have an odd number of students in class, you can call on a student to be the class helper of the day and help you pause the song in the first round. Then choose a second student to pause the song and have the helper participate, too.

WHICH LADDER IS JUST RIGHT TO SAVE THE CAT? LOOK AND CIRCLE.

STEAM • WHO LIVES AND WORKS IN MY TOWN? • UNIT 8   67

Learning goals
- Learn more about the work of firefighters
- Make a fire truck ladder and think of ways to improve it
- Measure the height of ladders and choose the ladder to save a cat

STEAM subjects
- Engineering
- Arts
- Math

Thinking skills
Remembering, understanding, applying, analyzing, creating

Main language content
Firefighters put out fires. They save animals from trees. They help people.
It's a small ladder. This ladder is just right.
Firefighter tools and transportation: fire engine, hat, hose, ladder, water
Numbers: 1-30

OPENING

Circle time

Materials and preparation
- A bell
- Puppet
- Visual schedule pictures

Say *hello* to students and invite them to sit in a circle. Encourage them to say *hello* to you and the puppet. Make it answer, *Hello, my friends.*
Then place the visual schedule pictures face down in the circle. Call on a student to turn over a picture and show it to the rest of the class. Elicit the name of the subject. Invite a student to make the bell chime and ask, *Can you hear the chime?* Elicit from the rest of the class, *It's (engineering) time!* Repeat with the other subjects.

Learn about firefighters.

Materials and preparation
- A book about firefighters (age appropriate, optional)
- Pictures of firefighters doing different tasks (watch out for violent scenes)
- Firefighter's tools or pictures of tools: a fire engine, a hat, a hose, a ladder, water

Bring a book about firefighters and read it to the class or show students the pictures you brought. Ask, *What do firefighters do?* Elicit, *They put out fires. They save animals from trees. They help people.* Have students give more details about how firefighters work, *How do firefighters save animals from the trees? Who would like to be a firefighter?*
Show students the tools and ask them what they think they are used for. If students use L1, rephrase their ideas in English in English.

70 STEAM

ACTIVE LEARNING

Engineering and arts – Make a new ladder for the fire engine.

Materials and preparation
- Masking tape
- Popsicle sticks (seven per pair of students)

Tell students that the ladder of the fire engine in your town has broken and now they need a new ladder. Ask, *Can you help? How can we build a ladder?* Allow students to be creative and express their opinion. Show the materials. Divide students into pairs and give each pair seven popsicle sticks and some pieces of masking tape. Have them figure out together how they can build a new ladder for the fire engine. Help those students who find it difficult to figure out a way of putting the popsicle sticks together.

Engineering – How can you make your ladder higher?

Materials and preparation
- Pieces of masking tape
- Students' craft ladders

Tell students that you sent a picture of the ladders to the firefighters and they found it too small. Say, *We have no extra materials. How can we make these ladders bigger?* Have students talk to each other. If they think of other materials, remind them that no new materials are available, only their own crafts. If students can't come up with the idea of joining two ladders and making a bigger one, have them work in groups of four and think together about the idea. As they test the ladder, help them use tape to attach the upper and lower parts. Encourage them to count how many popsicle sticks they used in all: *fourteen*.

> **Note to teachers**
> Having students reflect on their work and think of ways to improve it is a great way to introduce them to basic engineering processes.

DIFFERENTIATED INSTRUCTION

BELOW LEVEL
Math – Which ladder is just right to save the cat? Look and circle.

Materials and preparation
- Pencils
- Project Book page 67

Have students open their Project Book to page 67. Show them the ladders and elicit the word. Then have them count the ladders. Draw their attention to the picture of the cat and the tree. Ask, *What is the matter?* Encourage students to explain that the cat is in the tree: *It needs help. The firefighters can help, but they need a ladder.* Ask, *Which ladder is perfect for this tree?* Invite students to use a pencil to measure the height of the tree and the ladders and decide which ladder is best. Have them compare answers with a classmate.

ABOVE LEVEL
Have students do the procedures explained in *Below level*, but instead of using a pencil to measure the ladders, have them try to guess which ladder is just right for that tree, make a choice, and compare with a classmate.

CLOSING

Play *Crawl and go*. Say goodbye.

Materials and preparation
- A white sheet of cloth

Stay close to the door, open it, and wave the white sheet of cloth. Tell students the sheet is pretend smoke and they need to crawl under it and go through the door. Help them gather outside in the hallway in an orderly manner.
Wave goodbye to students and have them say *goodbye* to you.

> **Note to teachers**
> This game can teach students about basic safety measures when they see fire in a closed place. Explain this to students and show them the safety measures and signs around the school, such as the exits.

Notes

Notes

Notes

Notes

Notes

Notes

Notes

Notes

Notes